THE SWEARY INSULTS COLOURING BOOK

A foul-mouthed book
for foul-mouthed adults.

BY CAREN DUGDALE

Coloured by:

∘∘∘∘∘∘∘∘∘∘∘∘∘∘∘∘∘∘∘∘∘∘∘∘∘∘∘

Date:

∘∘∘∘∘∘∘∘∘∘∘∘∘∘∘∘∘∘∘∘∘∘∘∘∘∘

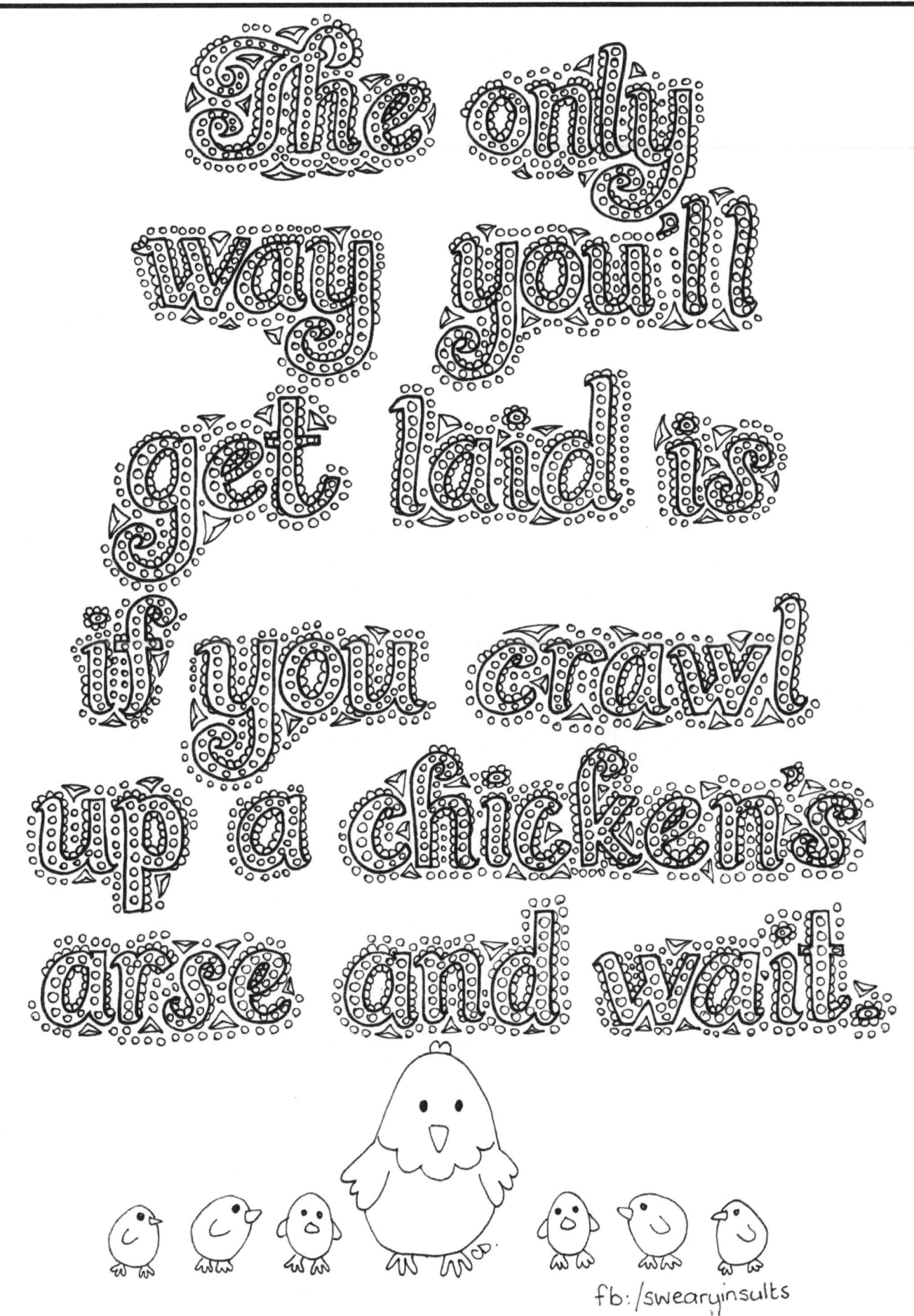

The only way you'll get laid is if you crawl up a chickens arse and wait.

fb:/swearyinsults

Coloured by:

° °

Date:

° °

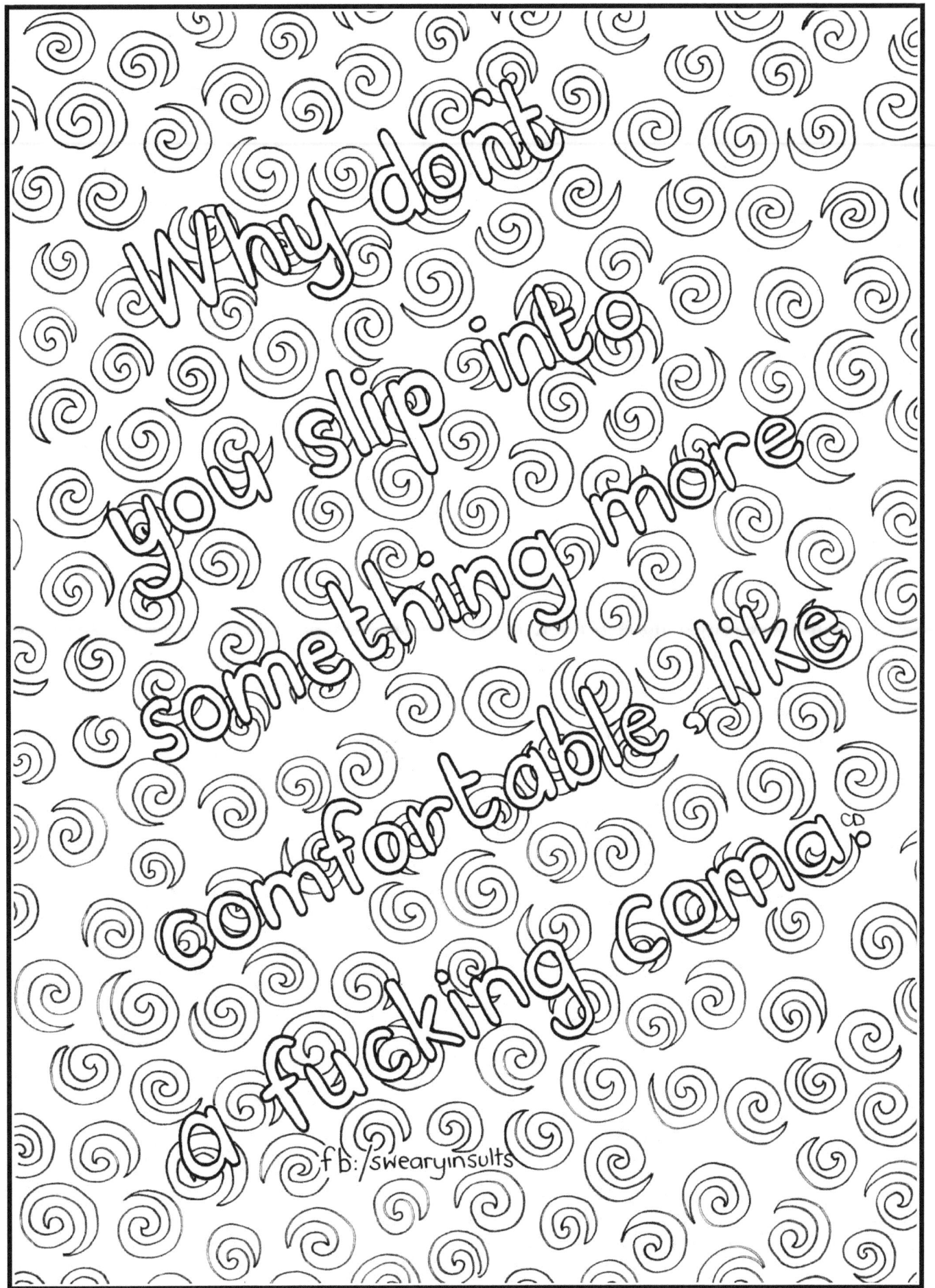

Coloured by:

○○○○○○○○○○○○○○○○○○○○○○○○

Date:

○○○○○○○○○○○○○○○○○○○○○○○○

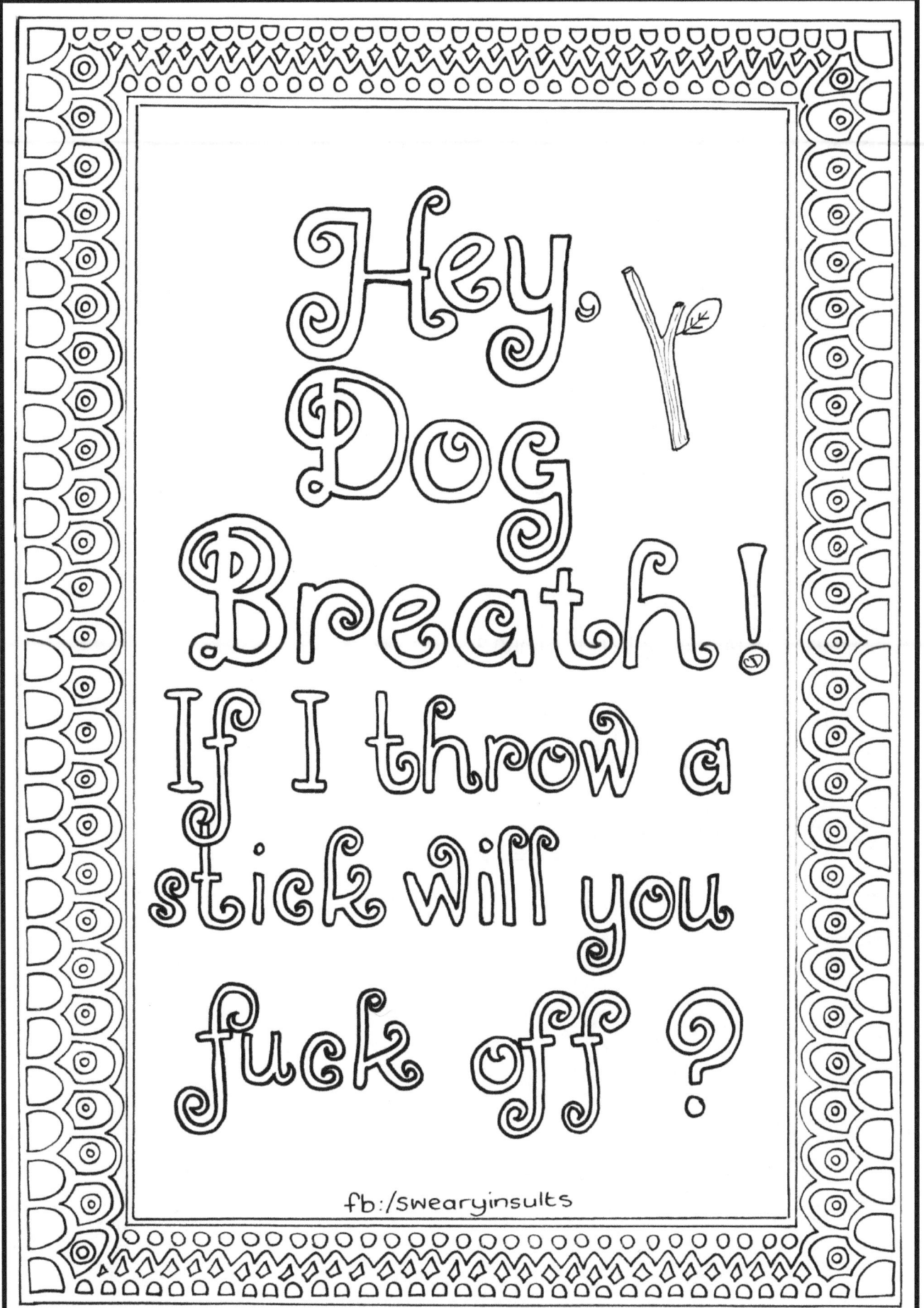

Hey, Dog Breath! If I throw a stick will you fuck off?

fb:/swearyinsults

Coloured by:

○○○○○○○○○○○○○○○○○○○○○○○○

Date:

○○○○○○○○○○○○○○○○○○○○○○○○

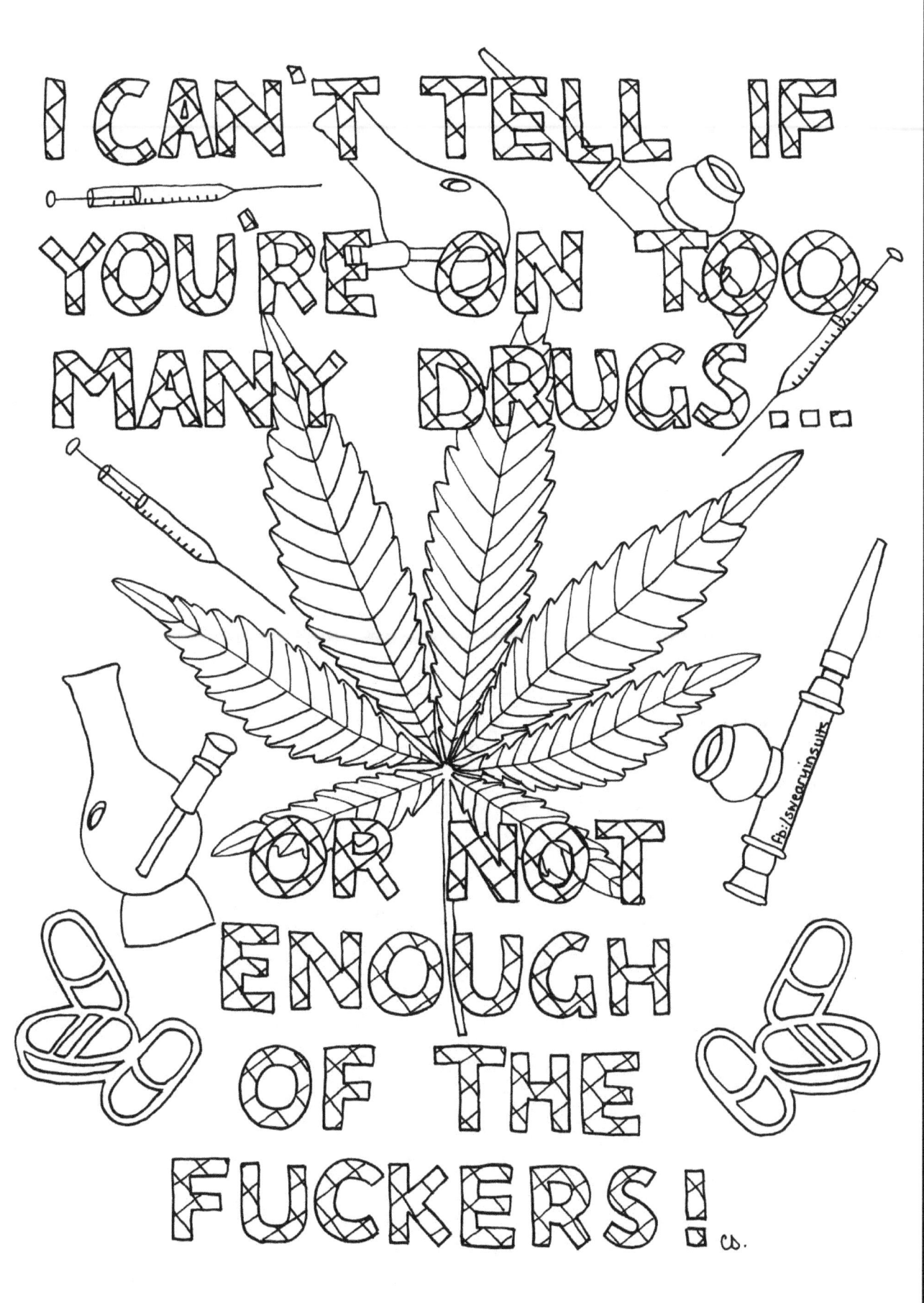

Coloured by:

○○○○○○○○○○○○○○○○○○○○○○○○

Date:

○○○○○○○○○○○○○○○○○○○○○○○

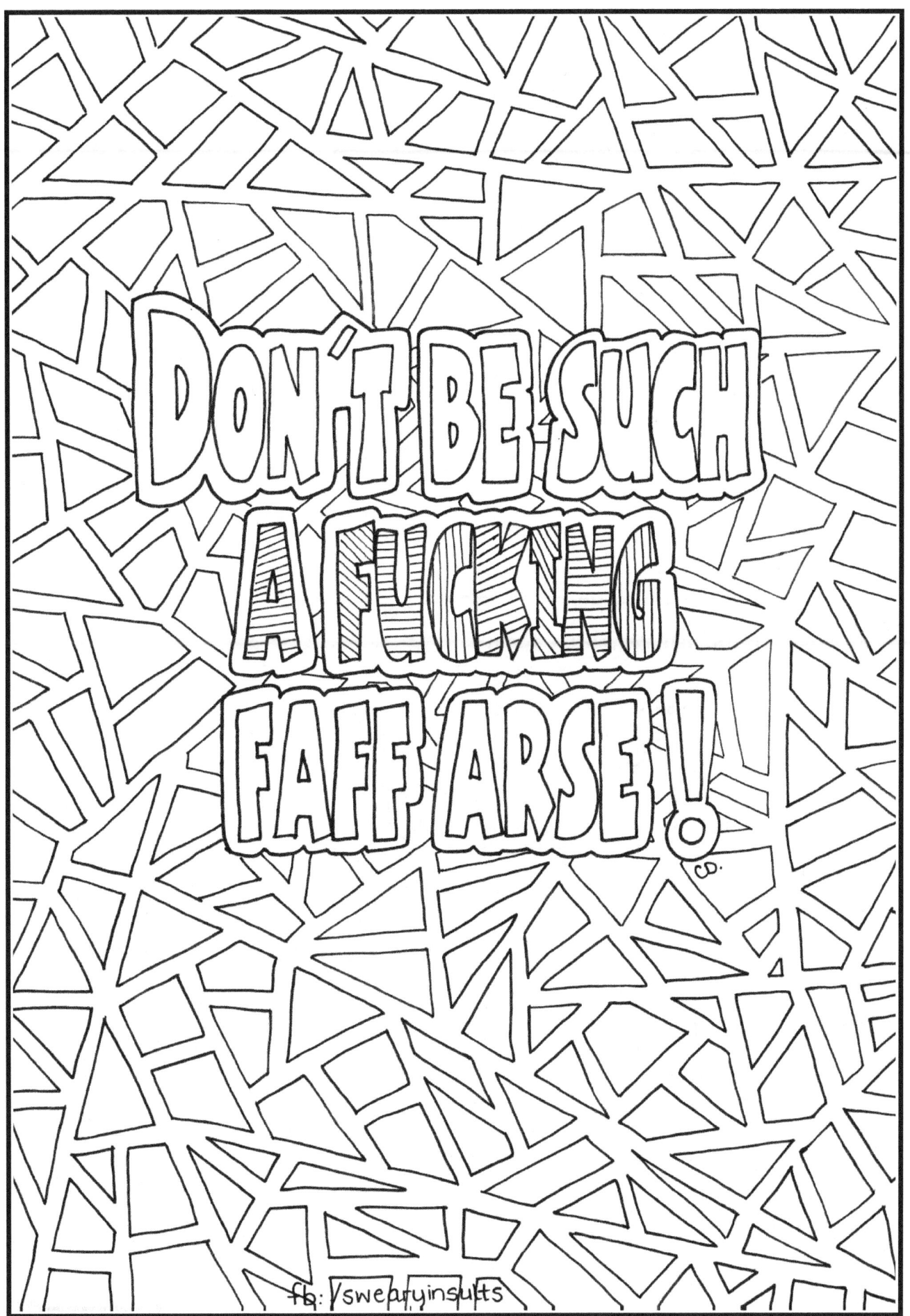

Coloured by:

○○○○○○○○○○○○○○○○○○○○○○○

Date:

○○○○○○○○○○○○○○○○○○○○○○○

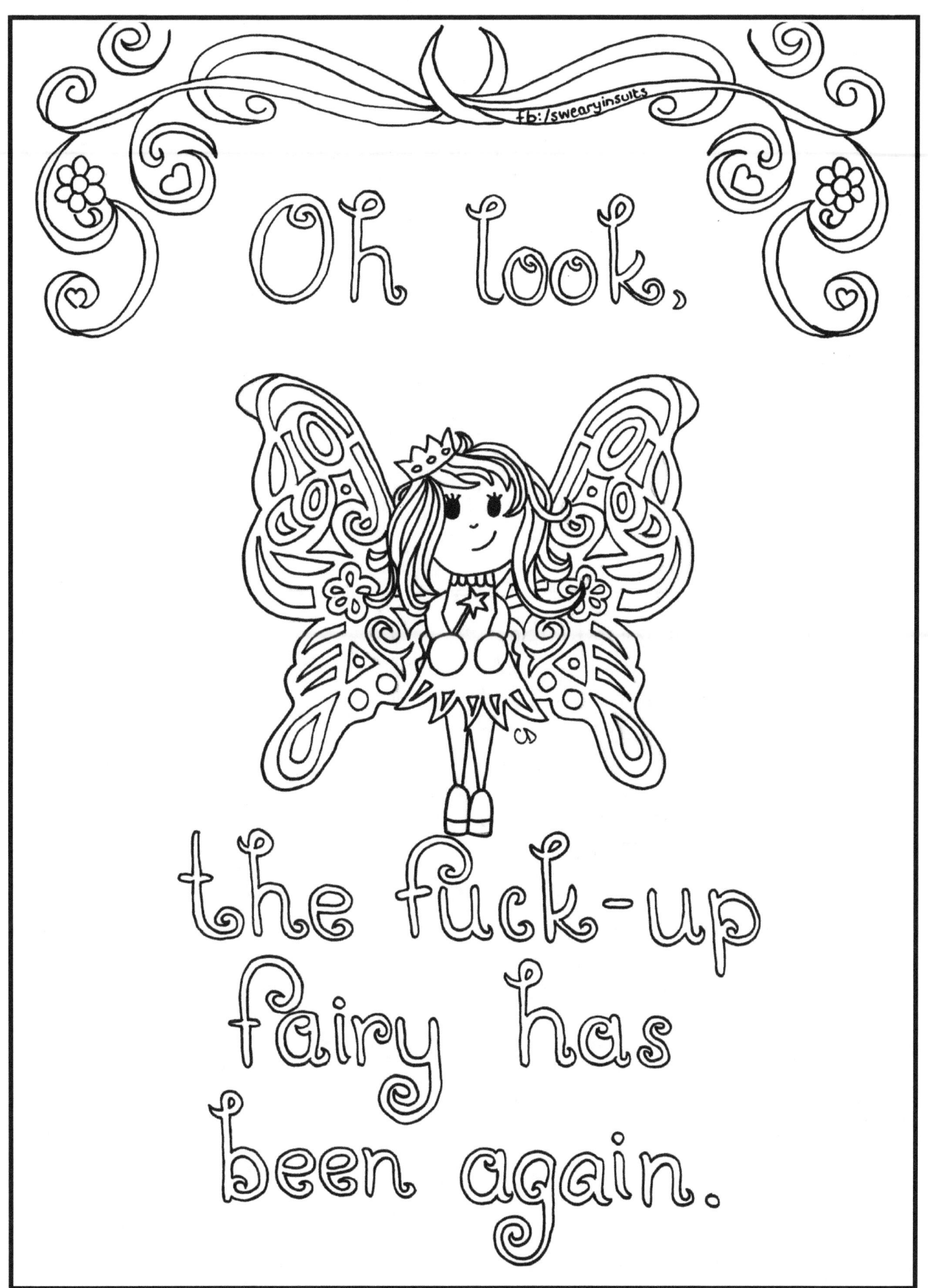

Coloured by:

○○○○○○○○○○○○○○○○○○○○○○○○

Date:

○○○○○○○○○○○○○○○○○○○○○○○○

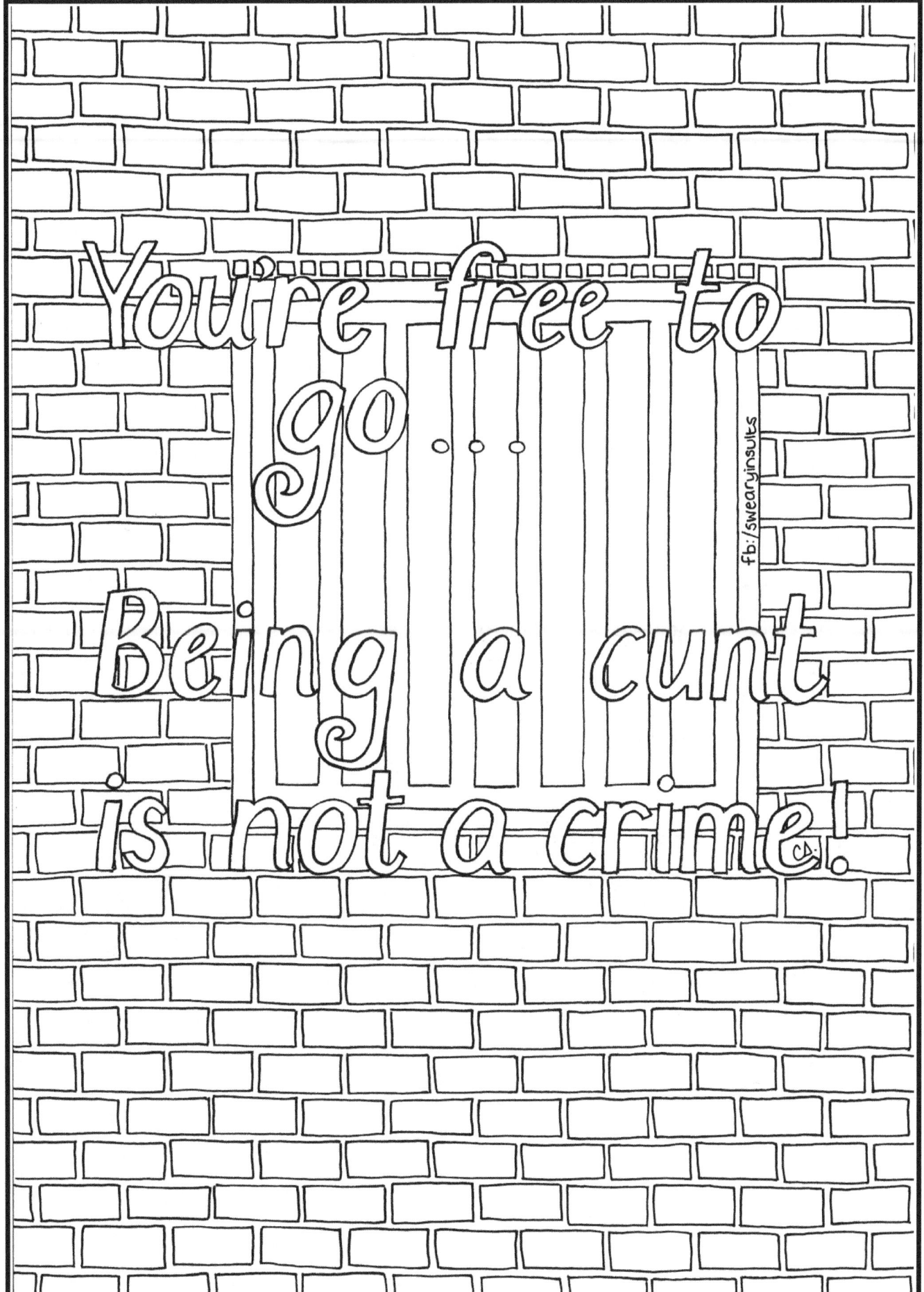

Coloured by:

○○○○○○○○○○○○○○○○○○○○○○○

Date:

○○○○○○○○○○○○○○○○○○○○○○○

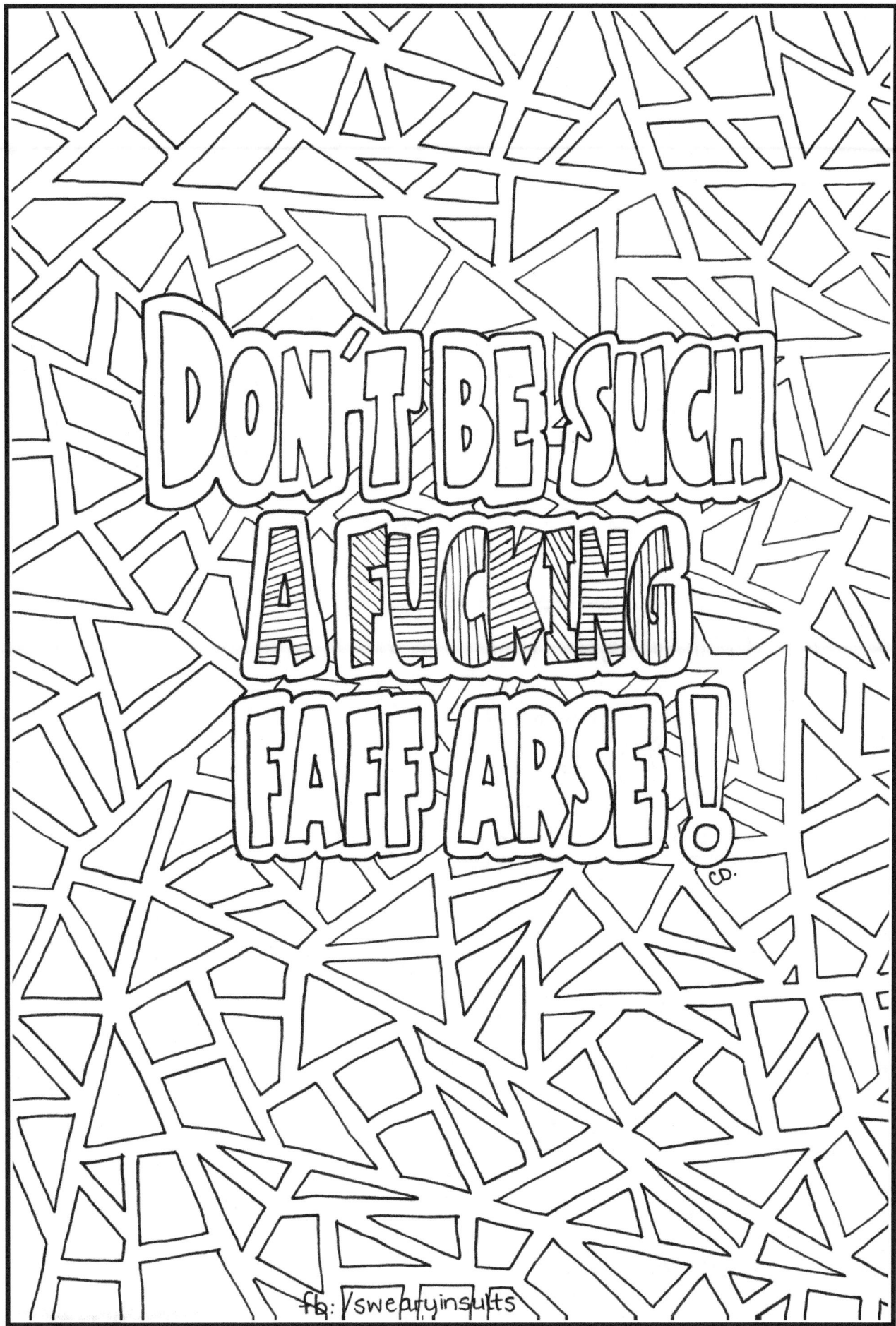

Coloured by:

oooooooooooooooooooooo

Date:

oooooooooooooooooooooo

fb:/swearyinsults

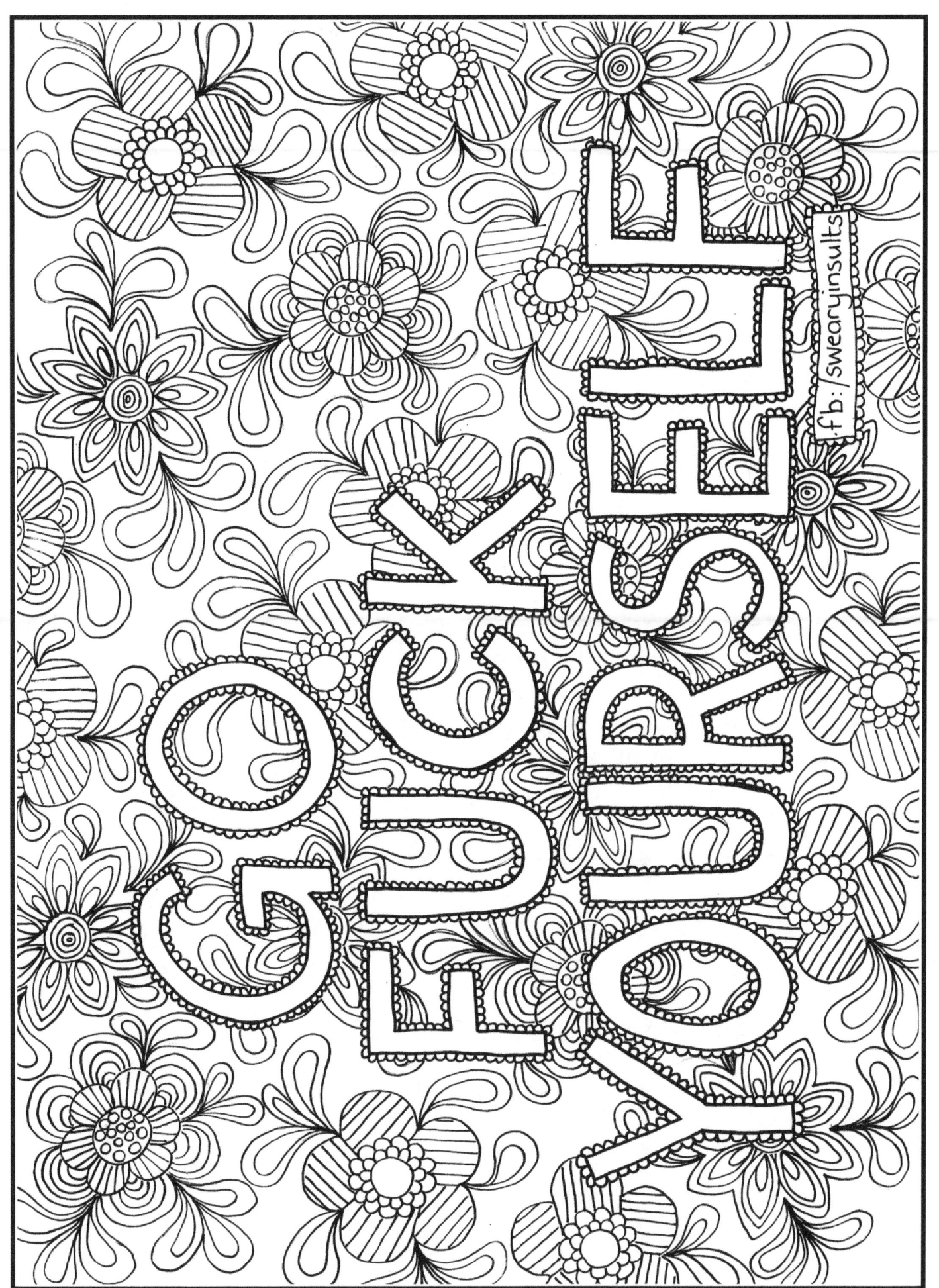

Coloured by:

∘∘∘∘∘∘∘∘∘∘∘∘∘∘∘∘∘∘∘∘∘∘∘∘∘∘

Date:

∘∘∘∘∘∘∘∘∘∘∘∘∘∘∘∘∘∘∘∘∘∘∘∘∘∘

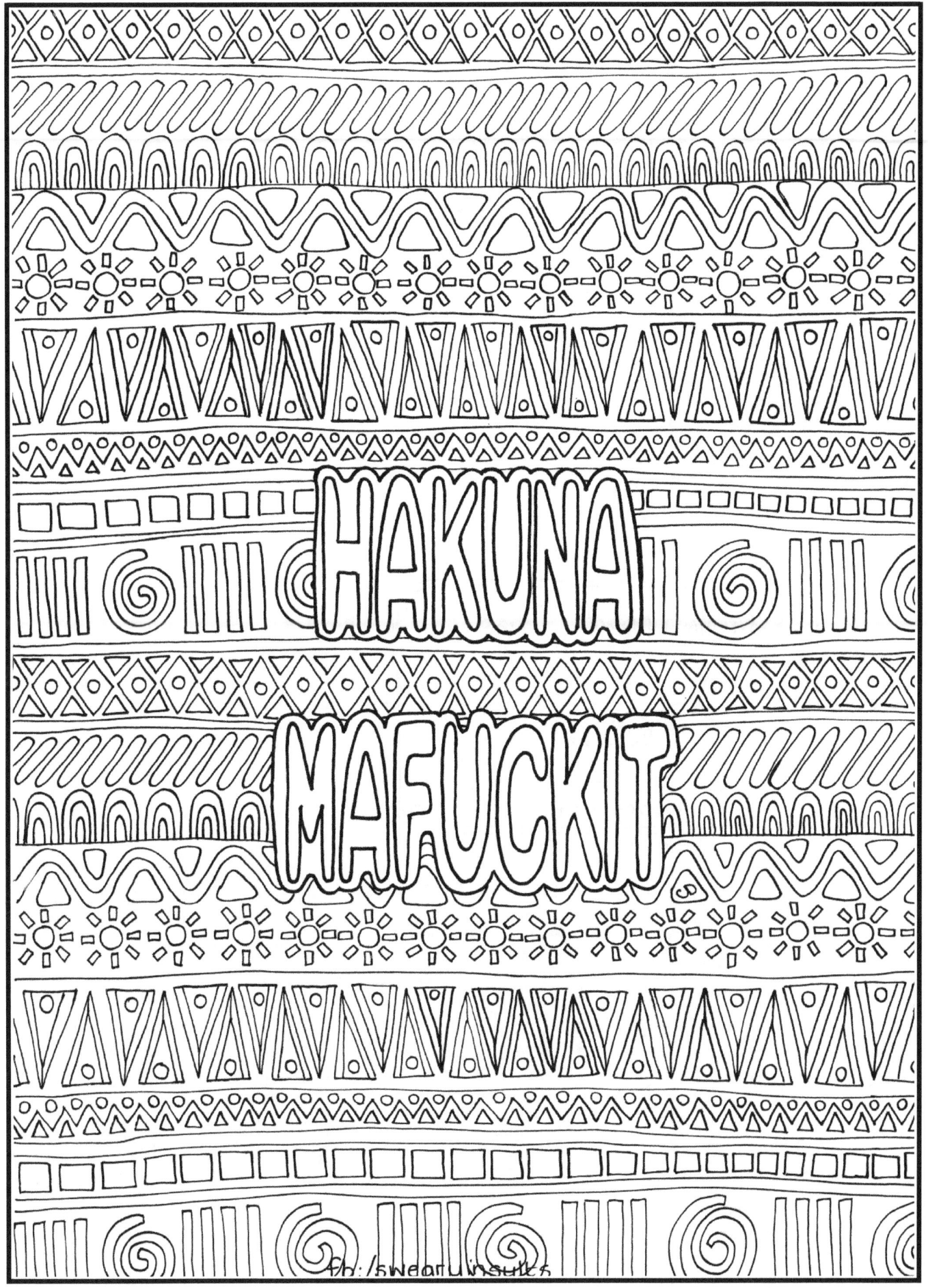

Coloured by:

o o o o o o o o o o o o o o o o o o o o o o

Date:

o o o o o o o o o o o o o o o o o o o o o o o

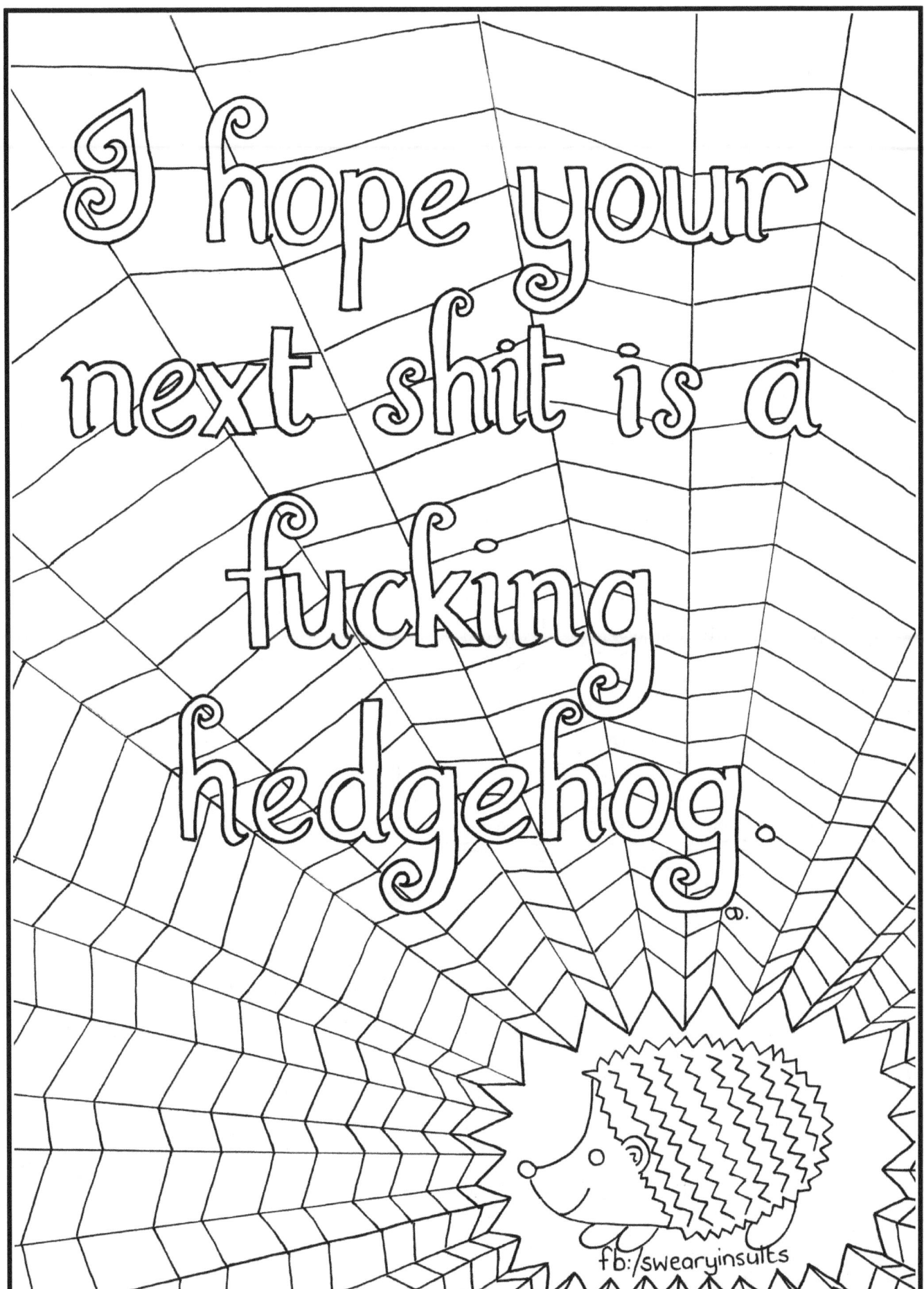

Coloured by:

∘∘∘∘∘∘∘∘∘∘∘∘∘∘∘∘∘∘∘∘∘∘∘∘

Date:

∘∘∘∘∘∘∘∘∘∘∘∘∘∘∘∘∘∘∘∘∘∘∘∘

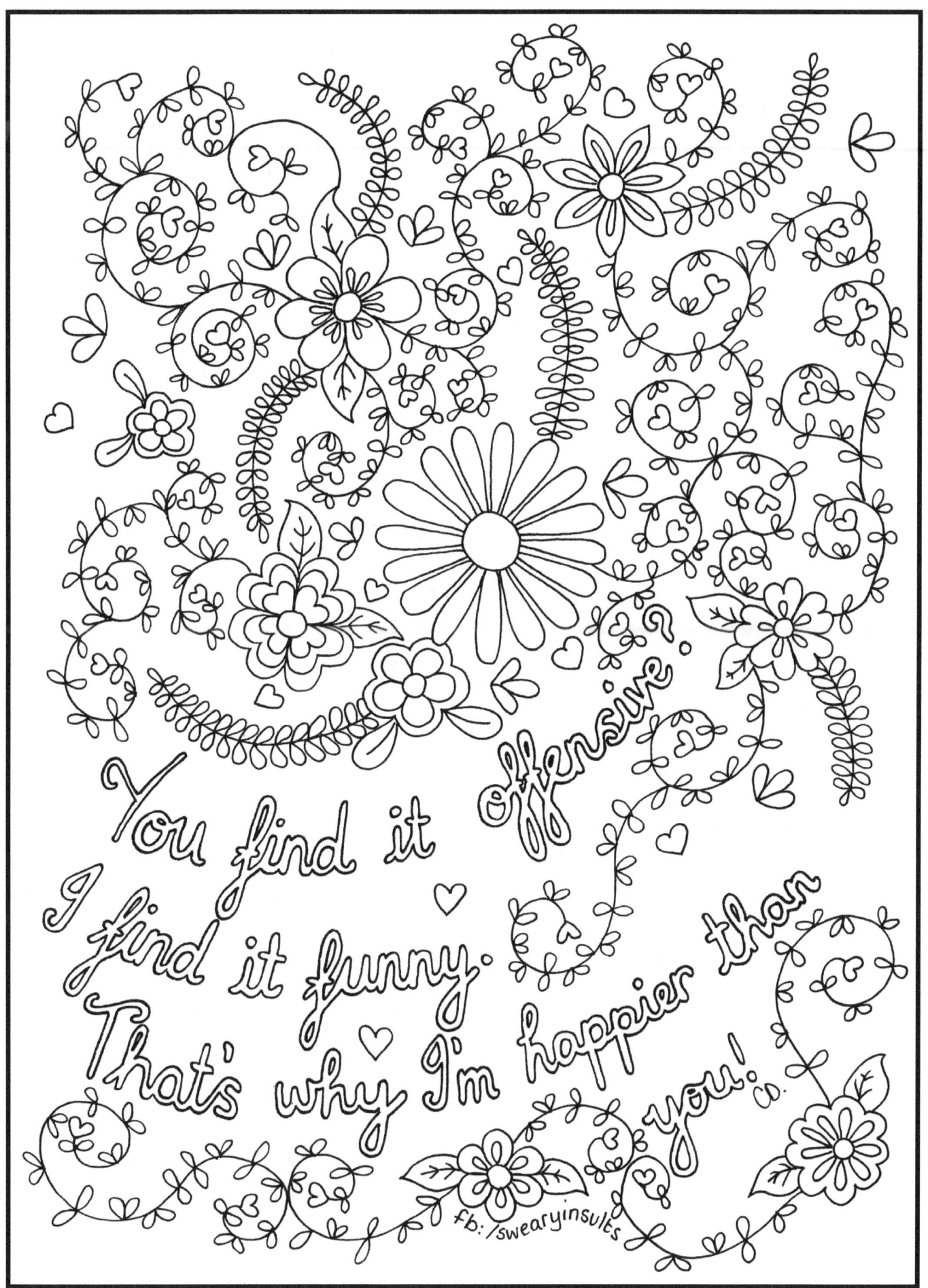

Coloured by:

○○○○○○○○○○○○○○○○○○○○○

Date:

○○○○○○○○○○○○○○○○○○○○○

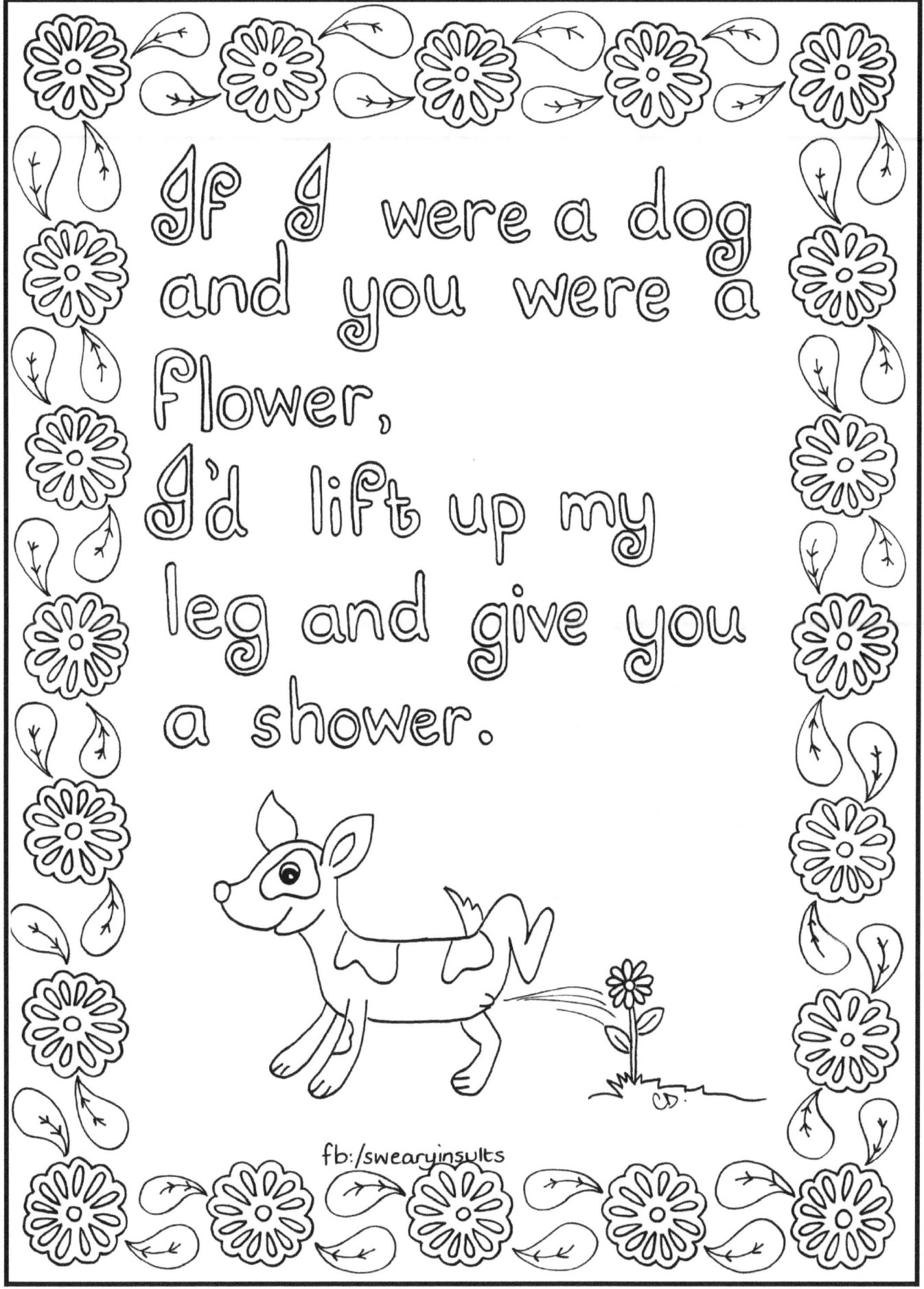

Coloured by:

∘∘∘∘∘∘∘∘∘∘∘∘∘∘∘∘∘∘∘∘∘∘∘∘∘

Date:

∘∘∘∘∘∘∘∘∘∘∘∘∘∘∘∘∘∘∘∘∘∘∘∘

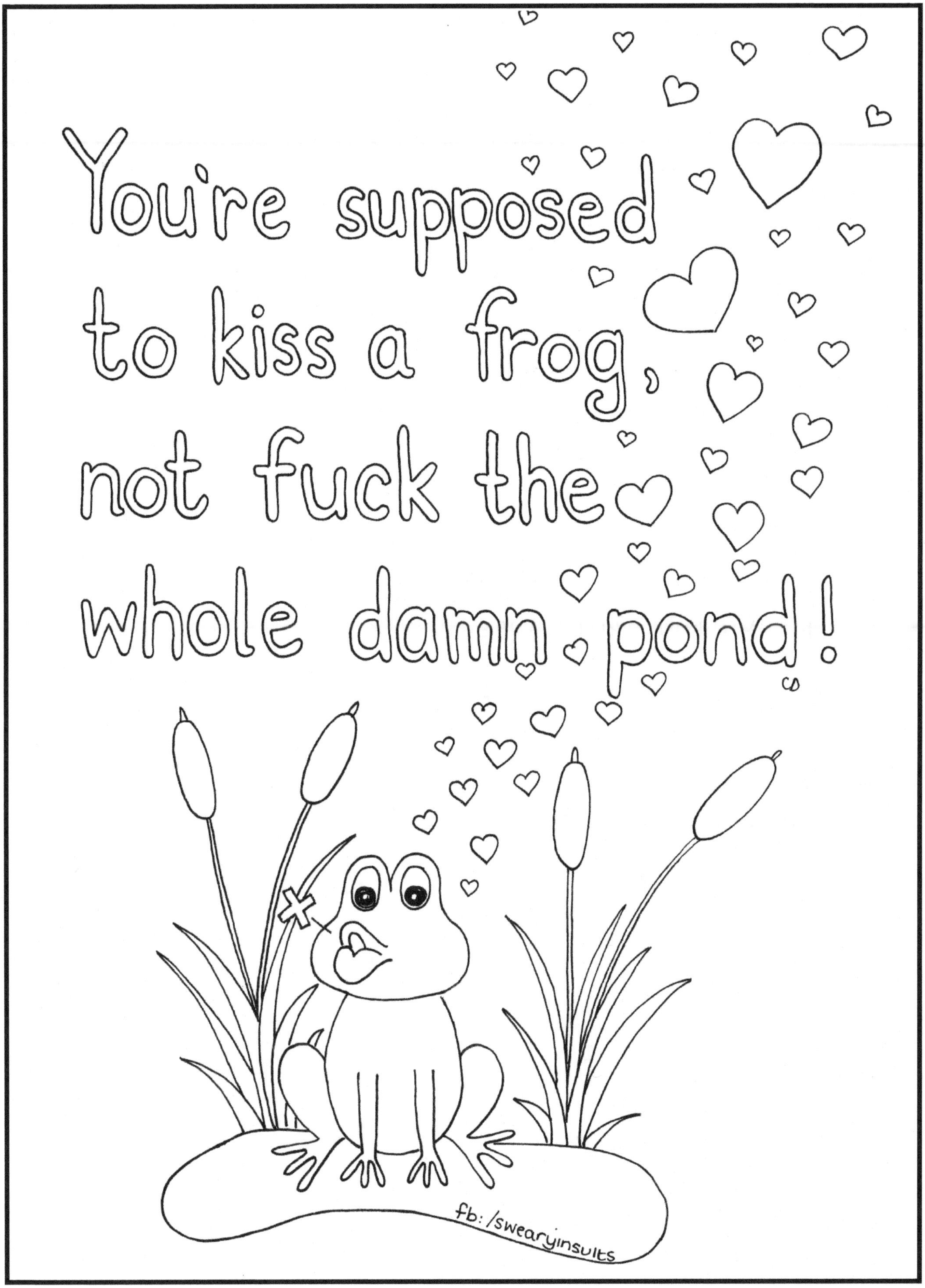
You're supposed to kiss a frog, not fuck the whole damn pond!
fb: /swearyinsults

Coloured by:

○ ○

Date:

○ ○

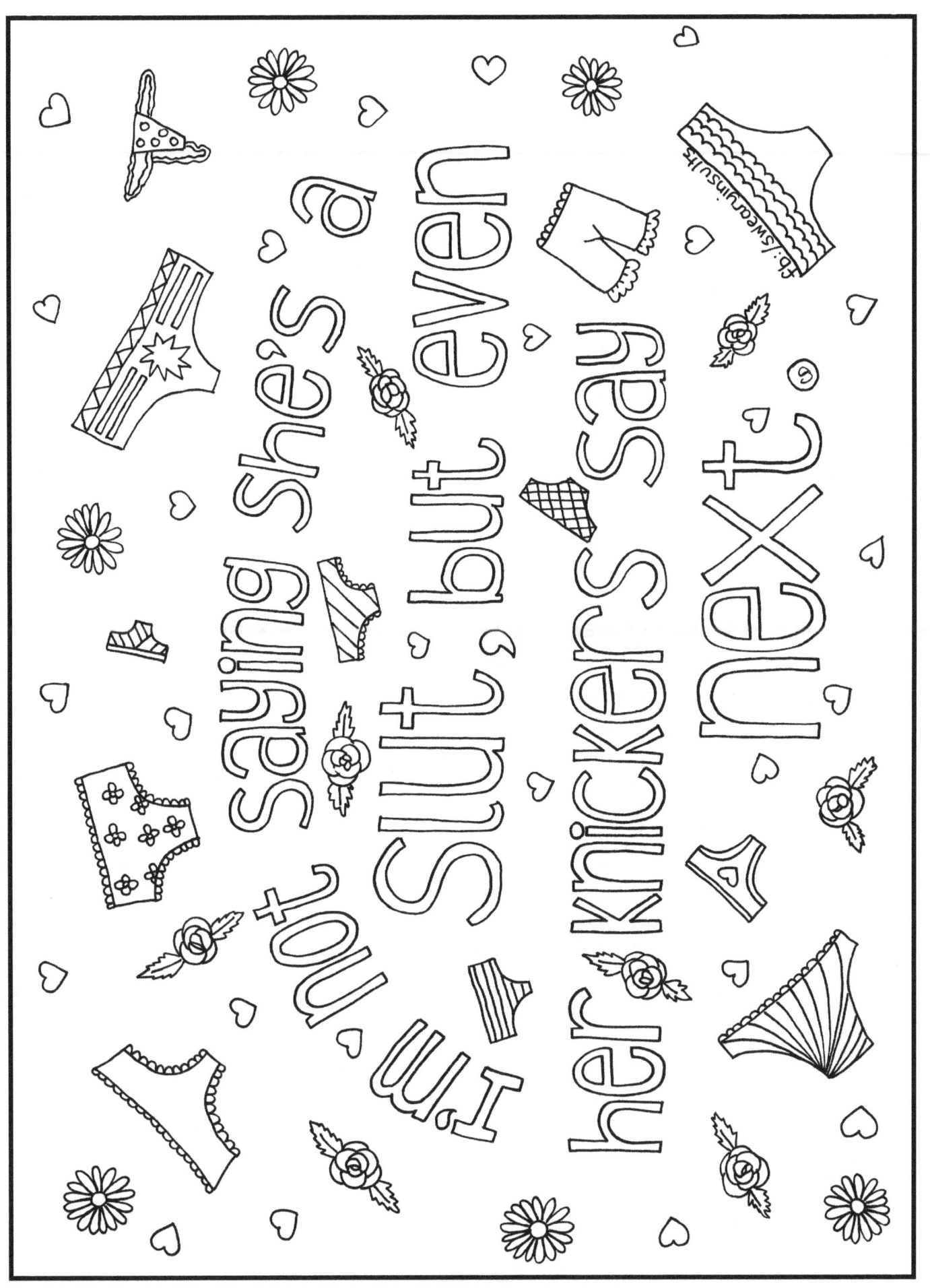

Coloured by:

○○○○○○○○○○○○○○○○○○○○○○○○○

Date:

○○○○○○○○○○○○○○○○○○○○○○○○

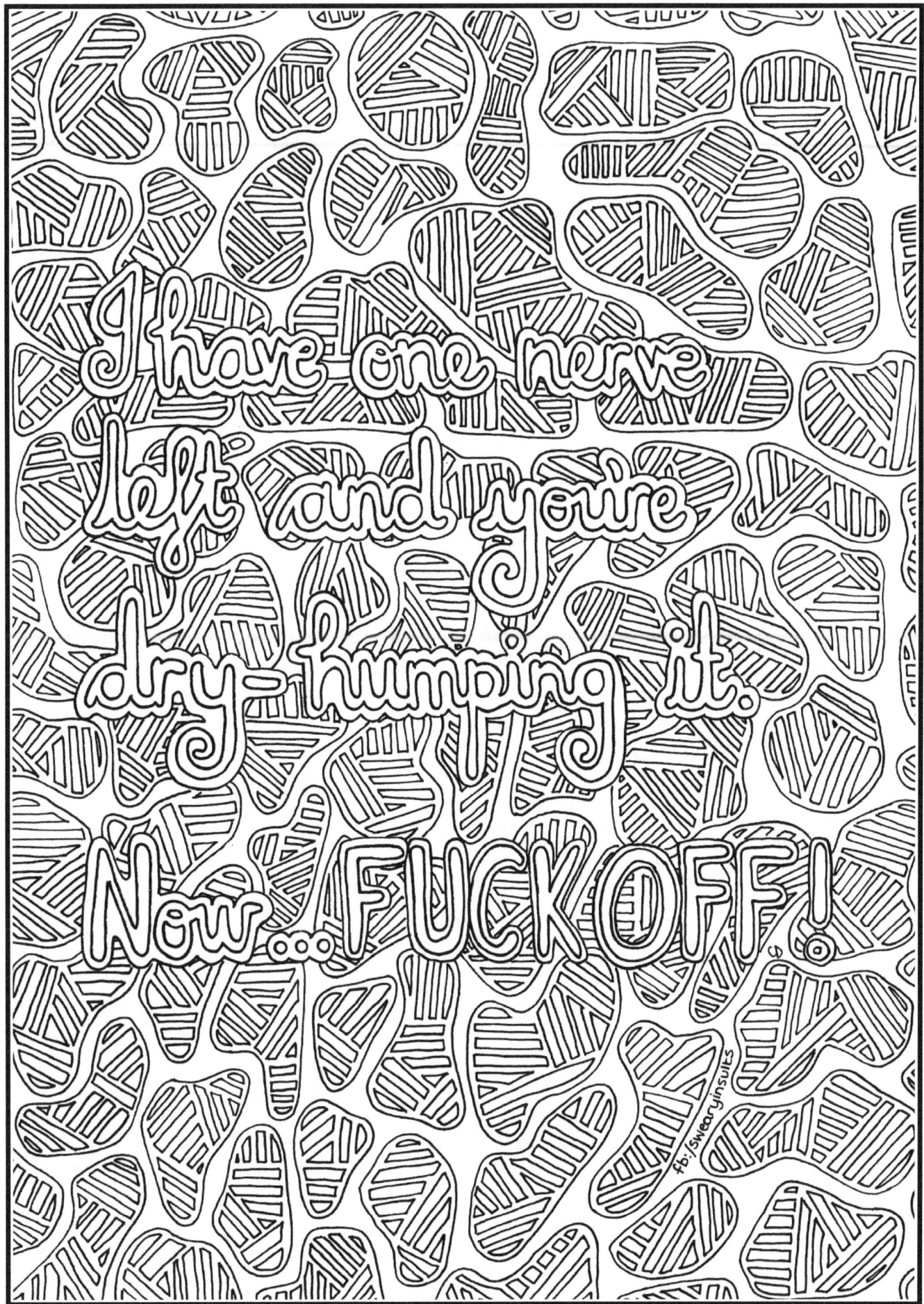

Coloured by:

○○○○○○○○○○○○○○○○○○○○○○○○○

Date:

○○○○○○○○○○○○○○○○○○○○○○○

i love to shop but i'm not buying this bullshit.

Coloured by:

○○○○○○○○○○○○○○○○○○○○○○○○

Date:

○○○○○○○○○○○○○○○○○○○○○○○○

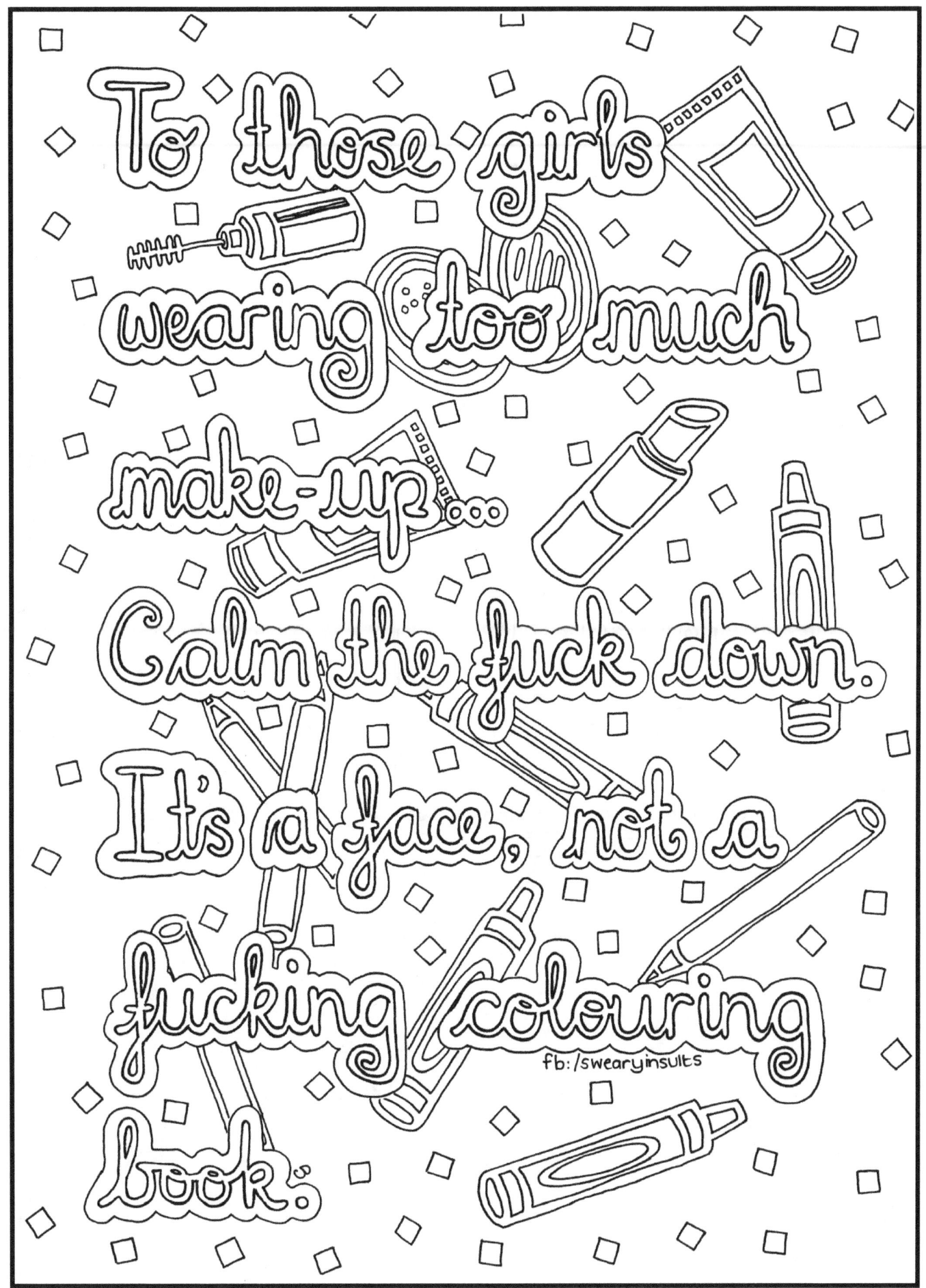

To those girls wearing (too) much make-up... Calm the fuck down. It's a face, not a fucking colouring book.

fb:/swearyinsults

Coloured by:

○○○○○○○○○○○○○○○○○○○○○○

Date:

○○○○○○○○○○○○○○○○○○○○○○○

CALM DOWN MONKEY TITS NOBODY GIVES A FUCK

fb: /swearyinsults

Coloured by:

○○○○○○○○○○○○○○○○○○○○○○

Date:

○○○○○○○○○○○○○○○○○○○○○○○

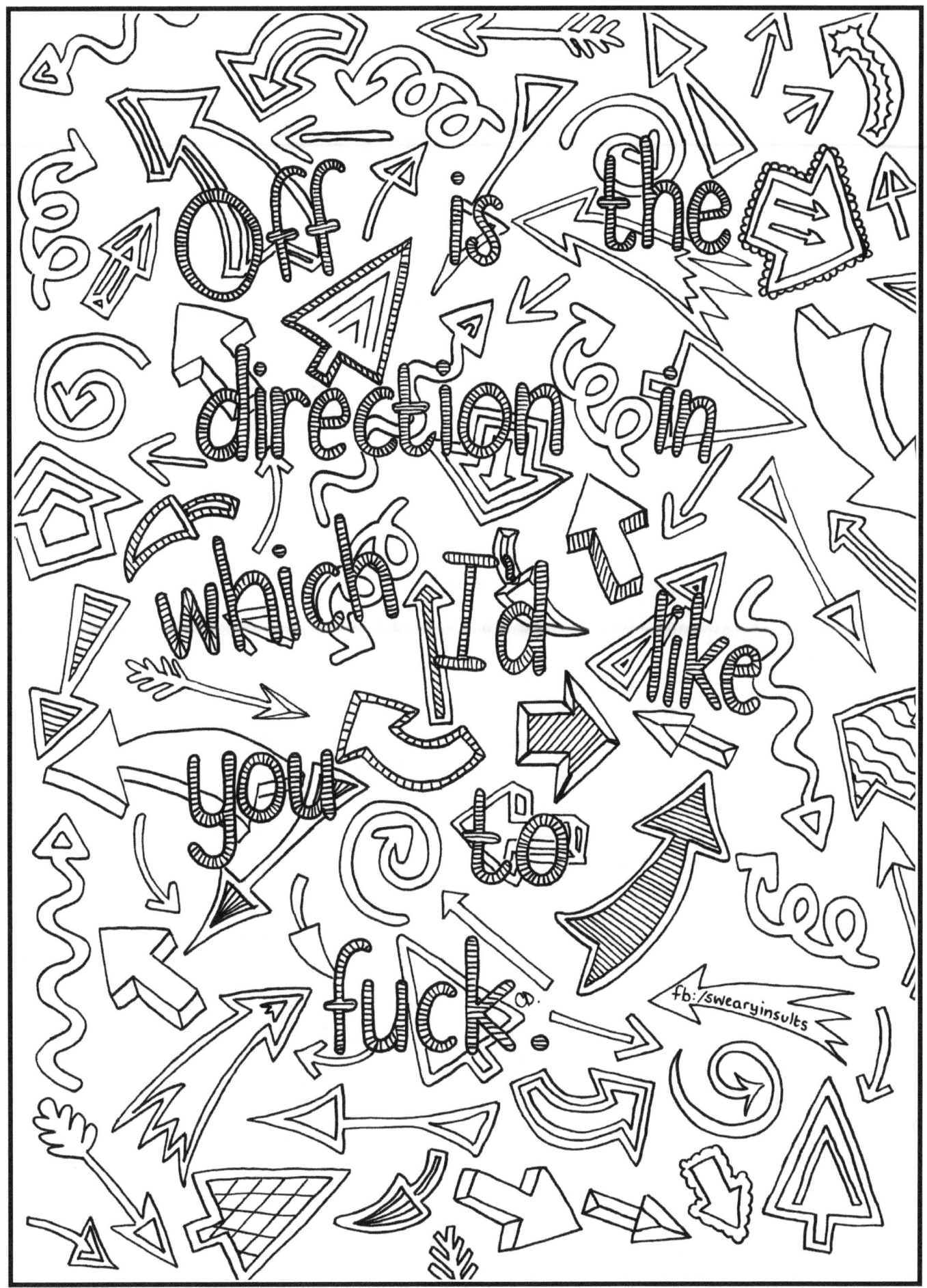

Coloured by:

○ ○

Date:

○ ○

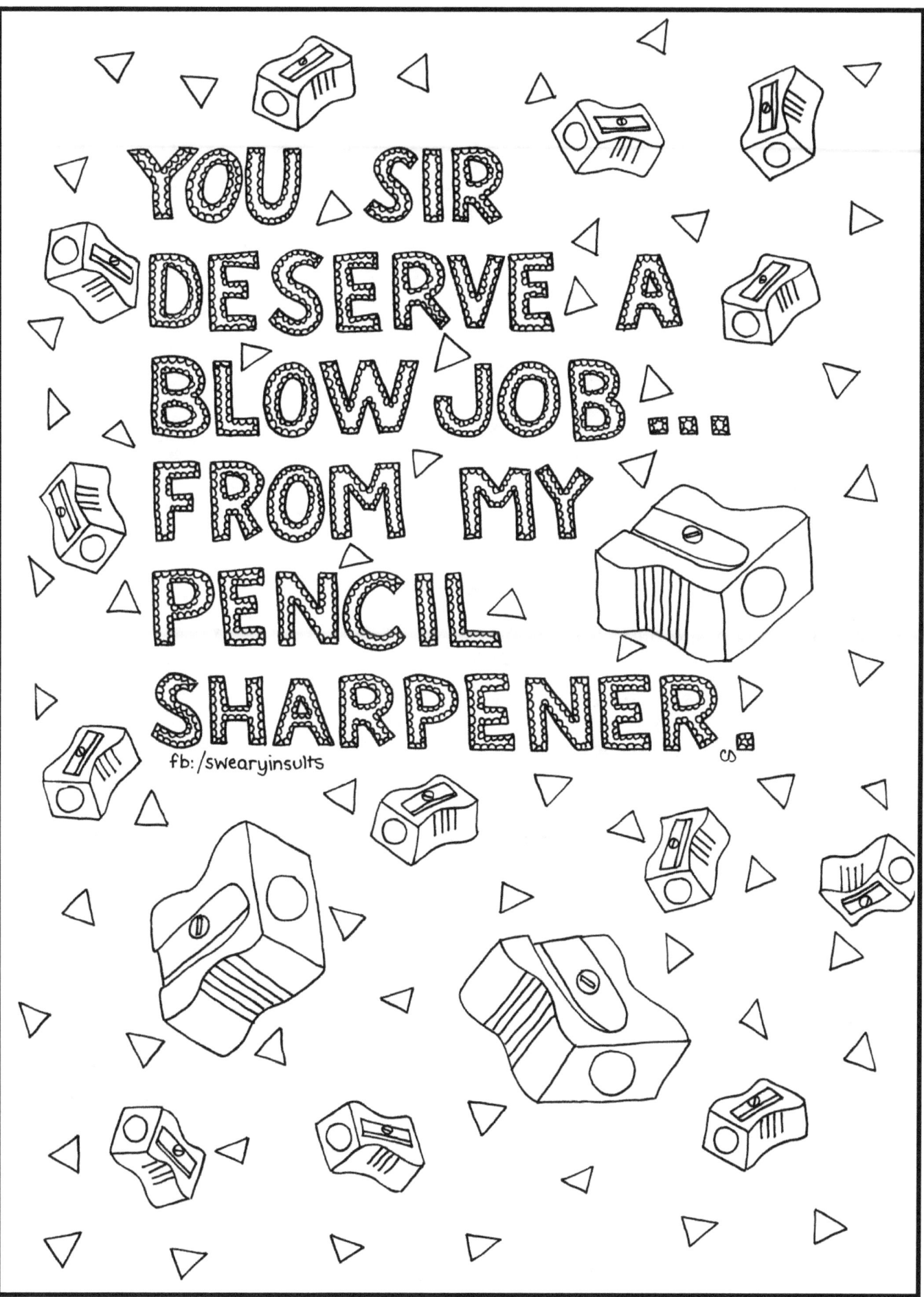

Coloured by:

° °

Date:

° °

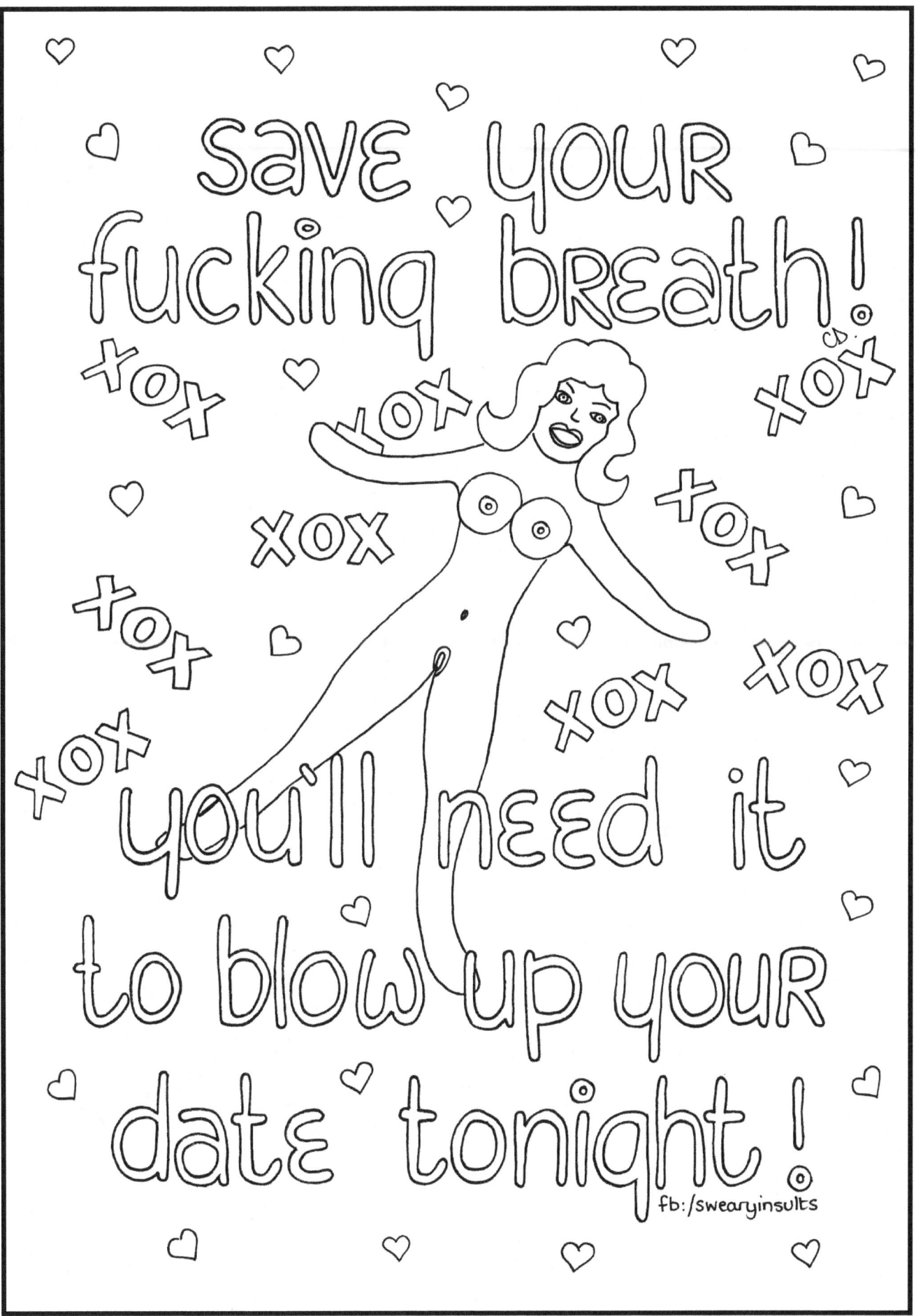

Coloured by:

○○○○○○○○○○○○○○○○○○○○○○○○○

Date:

○○○○○○○○○○○○○○○○○○○○○○○

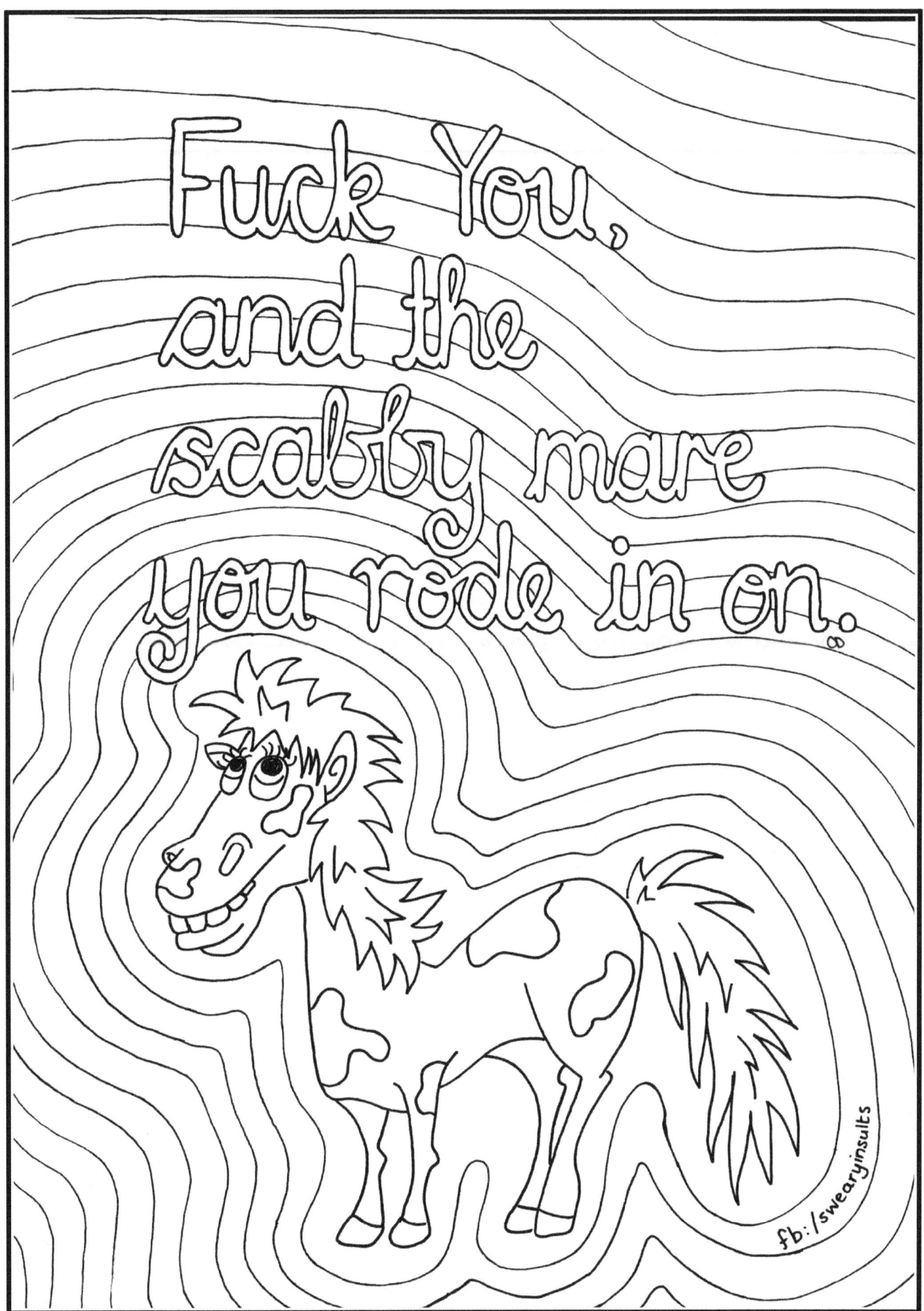

Coloured by:

○ ○

Date:

○ ○

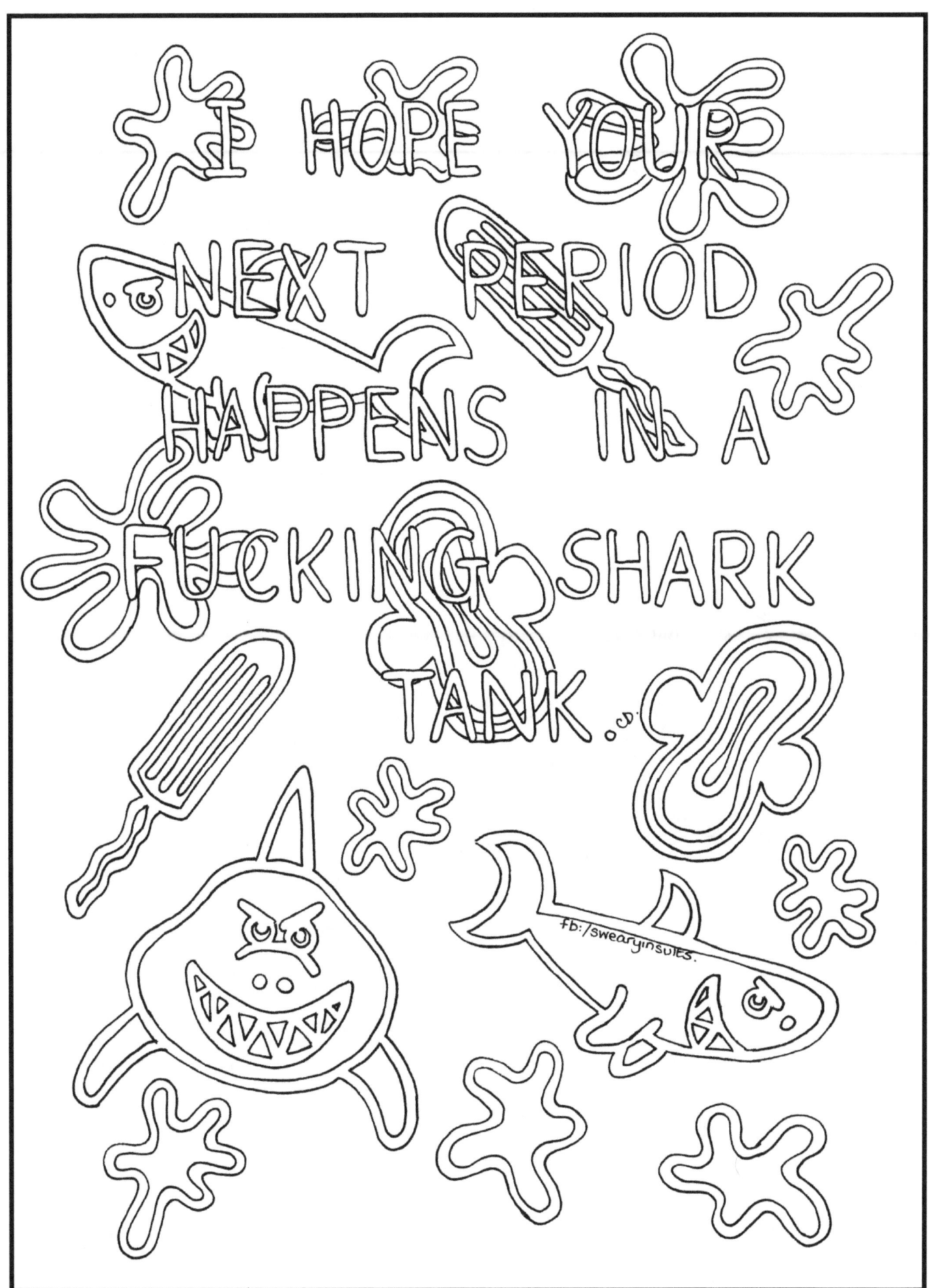

Coloured by:

∘∘∘∘∘∘∘∘∘∘∘∘∘∘∘∘∘∘∘∘∘∘∘

Date:

∘∘∘∘∘∘∘∘∘∘∘∘∘∘∘∘∘∘∘∘∘∘

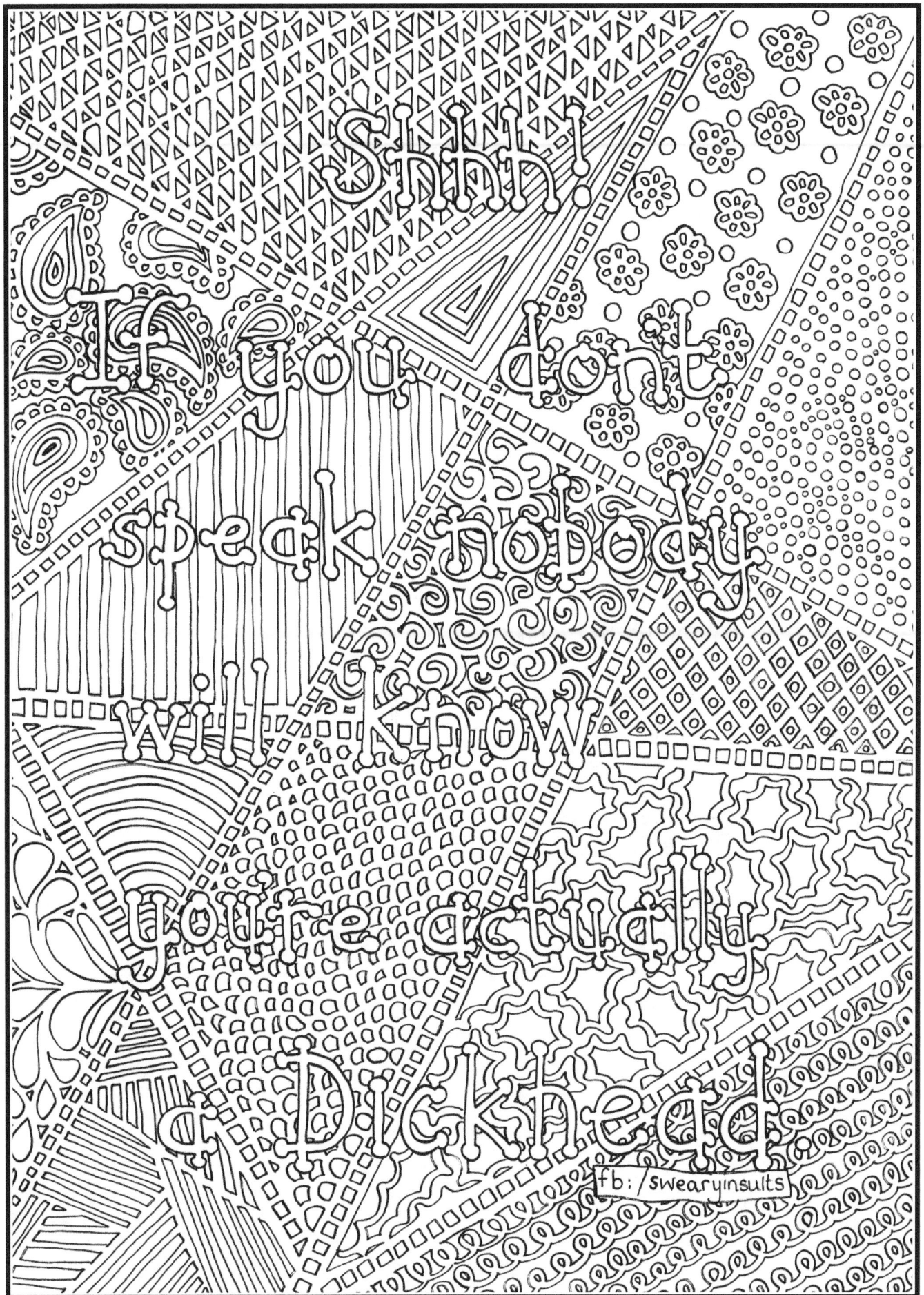

Coloured by:

○ ○

Date:

○ ○

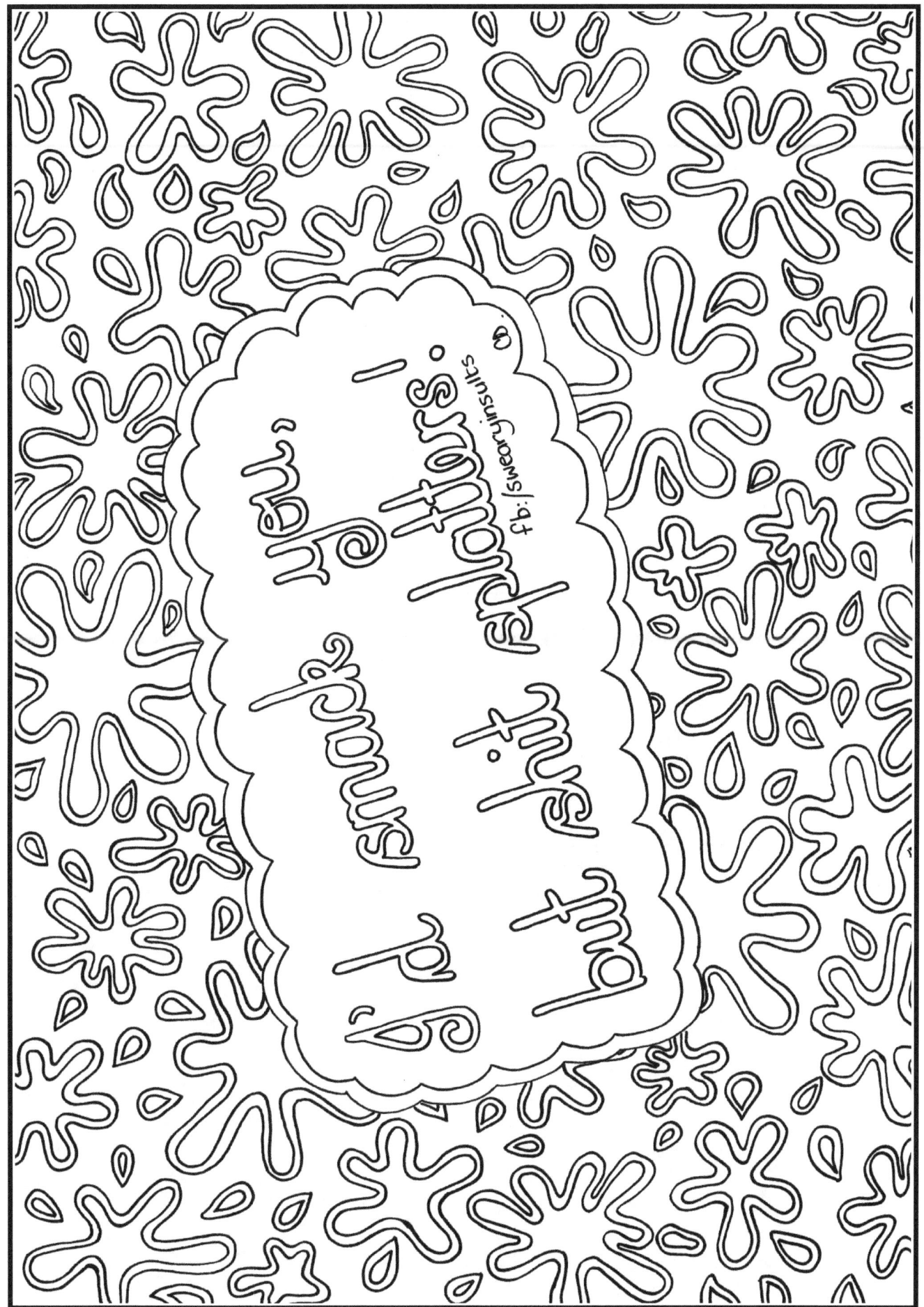

Coloured by:

○○○○○○○○○○○○○○○○○○○○○○○○○○

Date:

○○○○○○○○○○○○○○○○○○○○○○○○

fb:/swearyinsults

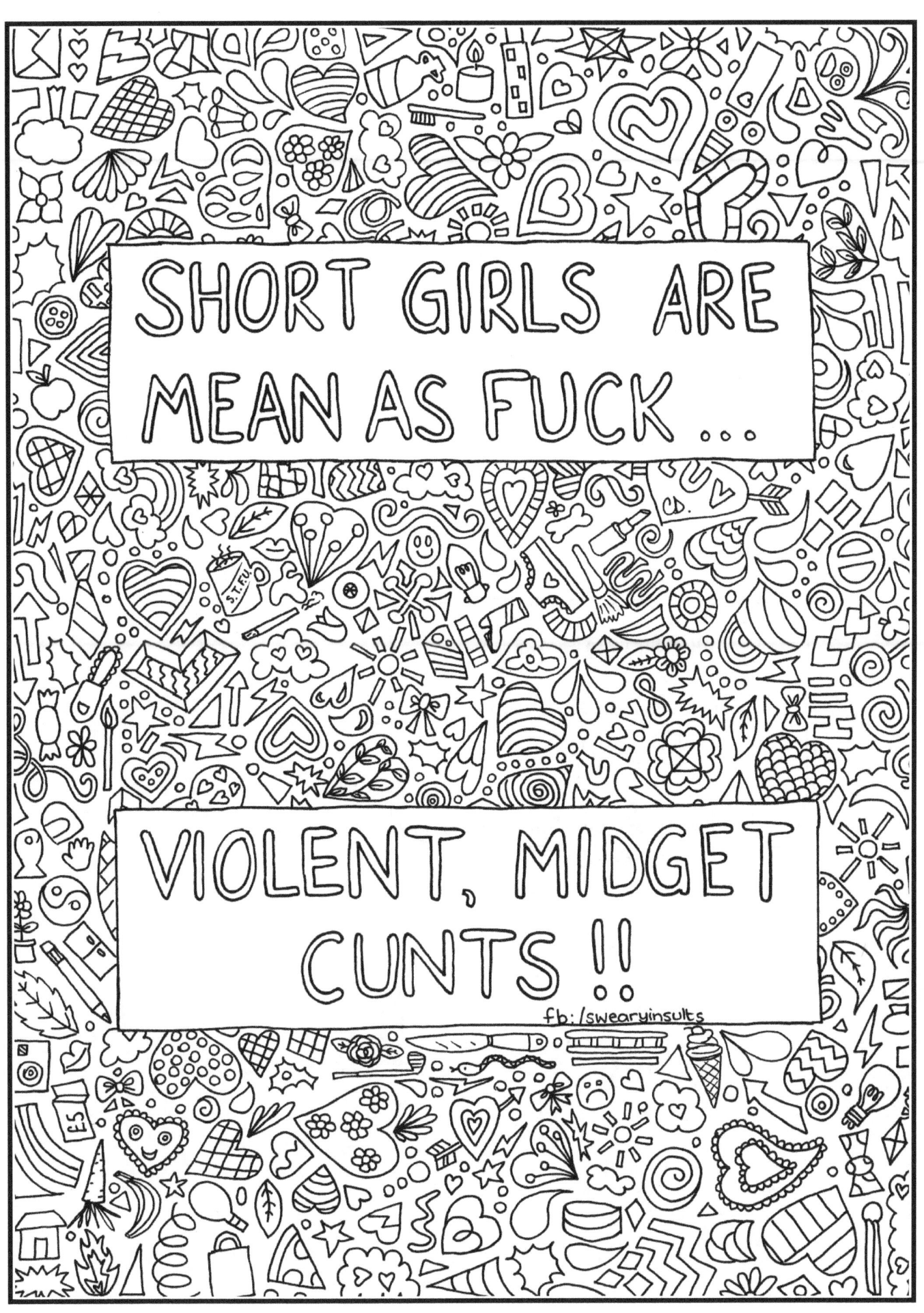

Coloured by:

○○○○○○○○○○○○○○○○○○○○○○

Date:

○○○○○○○○○○○○○○○○○○○○○○○○

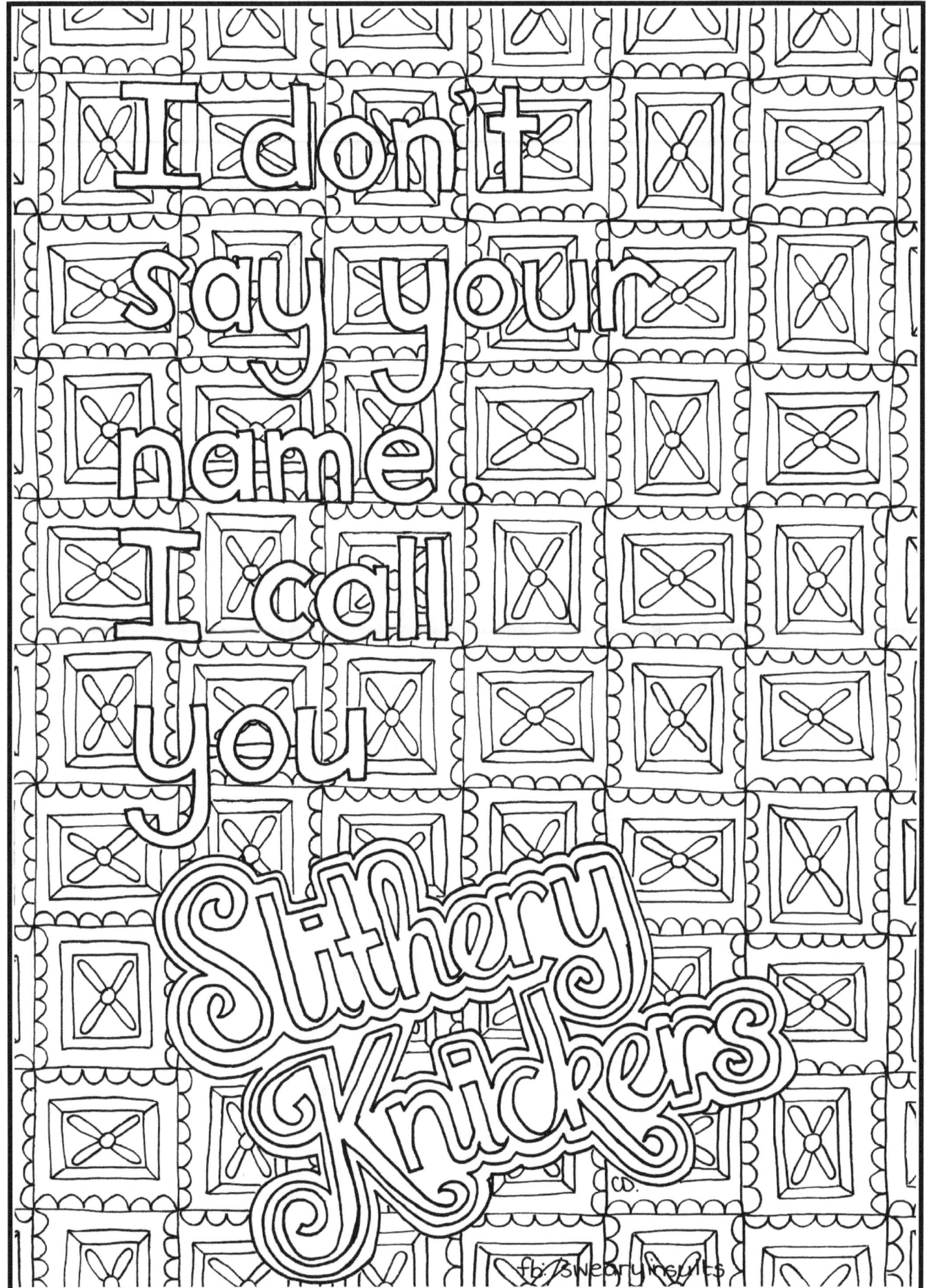

Coloured by:

○○○○○○○○○○○○○○○○○○○○○○○○

Date:

○○○○○○○○○○○○○○○○○○○○○○○

YOU FELL FROM THE TOP OF THE SLUT TREE AND BANGED EVERY GUY ON THE WAY DOWN.

Coloured by:

° °

Date:

° °

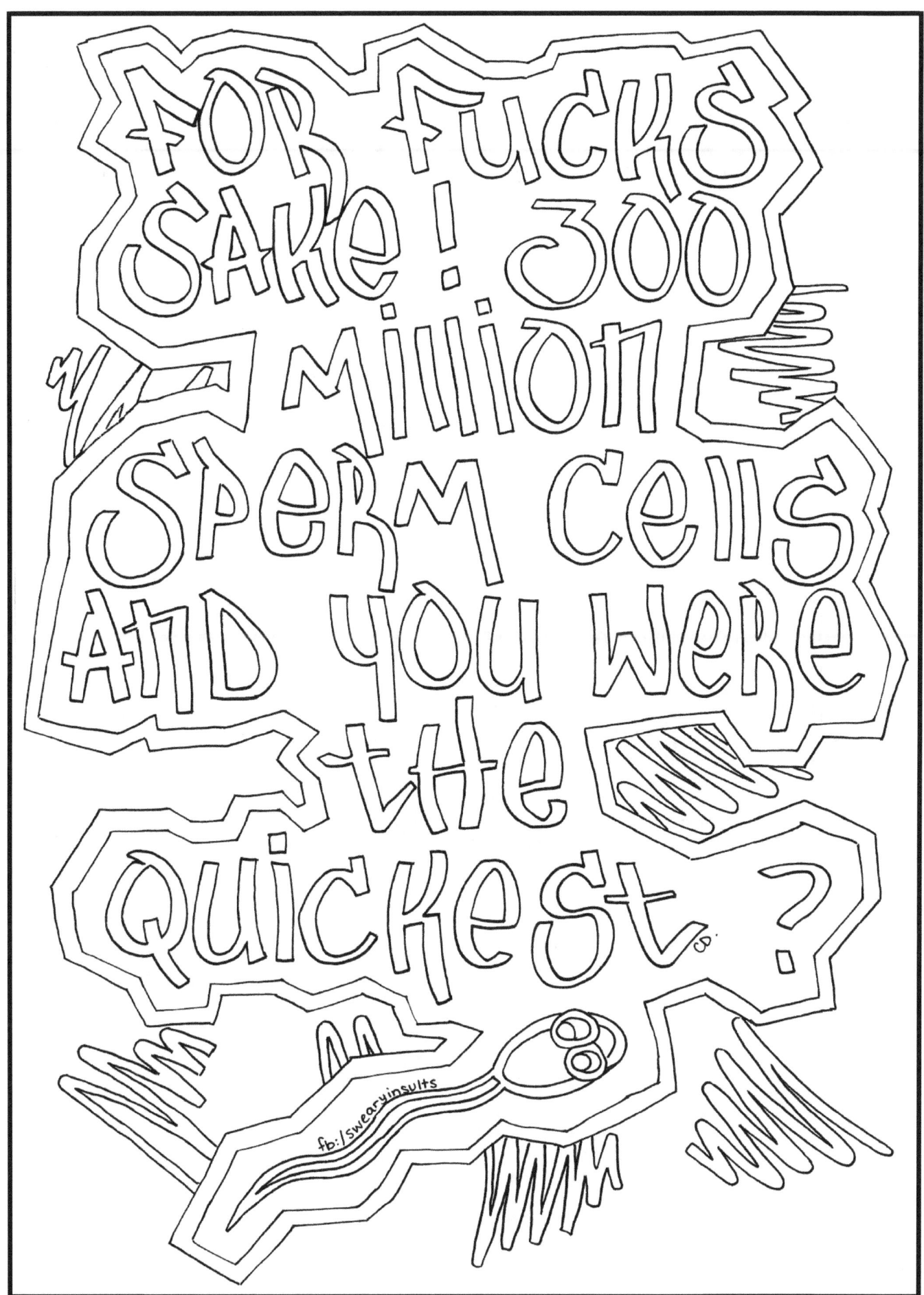

Coloured by:

○○○○○○○○○○○○○○○○○○○○○○○○

Date:

○○○○○○○○○○○○○○○○○○○○○○

fb:/swearyinsults

Keep your fucking WHORE HOLE Shut, you SKANKARONI SWAMP DONKEY SLUT.

Coloured by:

○ ○

Date:

○ ○

fb:/swearyinsults

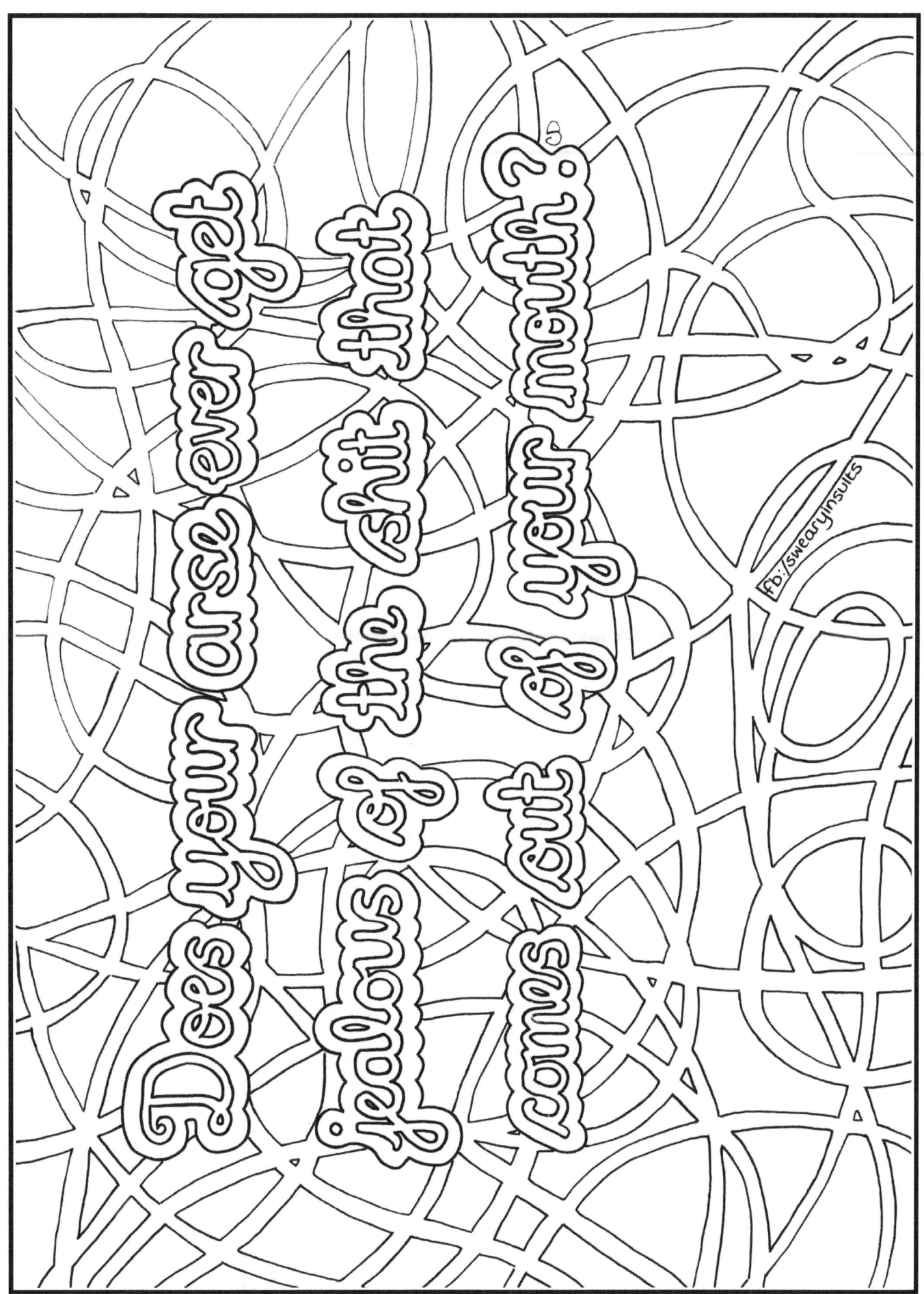

Coloured by:

° °

Date:

° °

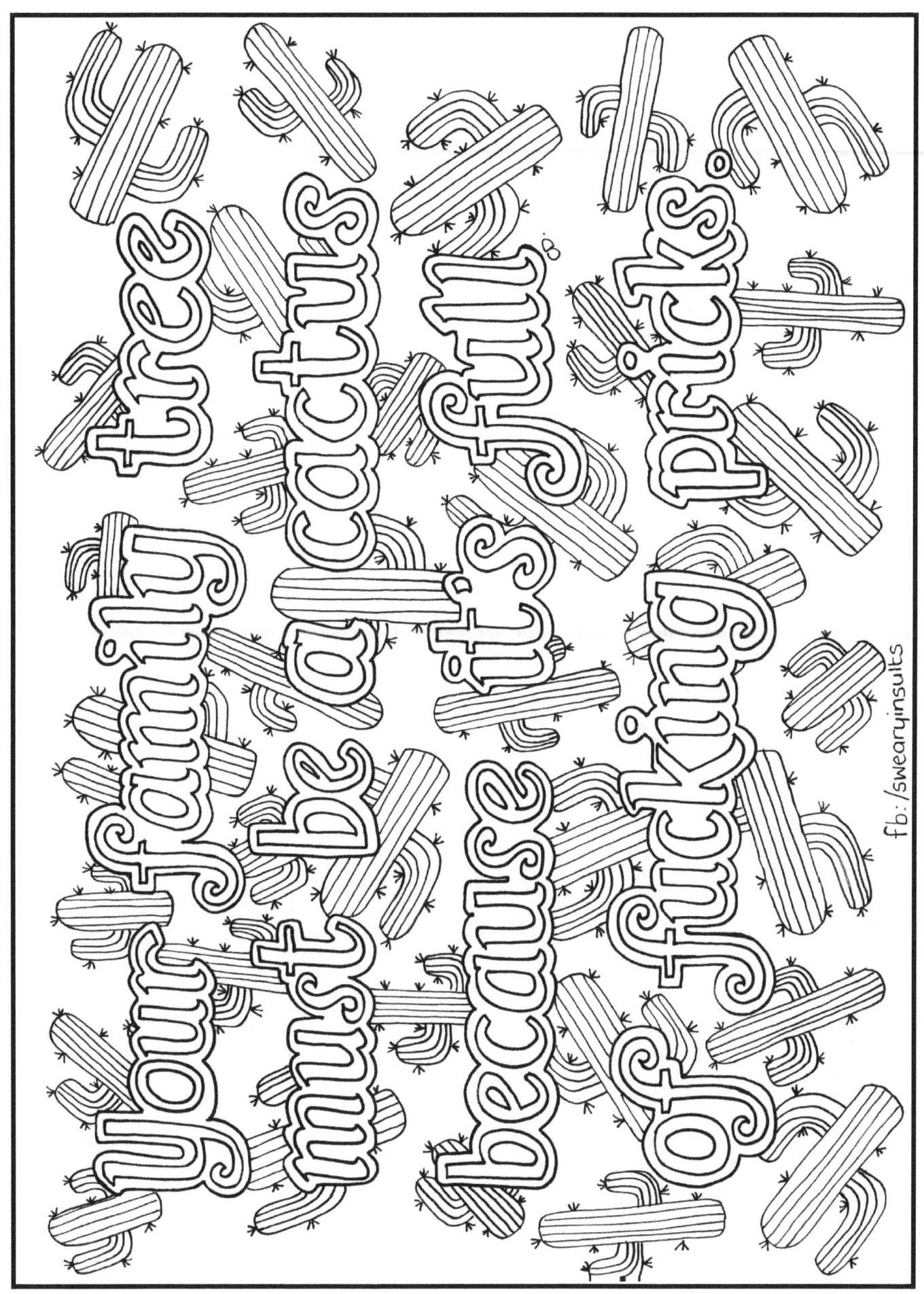

your family tree must be a cactus because it's full fucking so fucking pricks.

Coloured by:

o o o o o o o o o o o o o o o o o o o o o o o

Date:

o o o o o o o o o o o o o o o o o o o o o o o

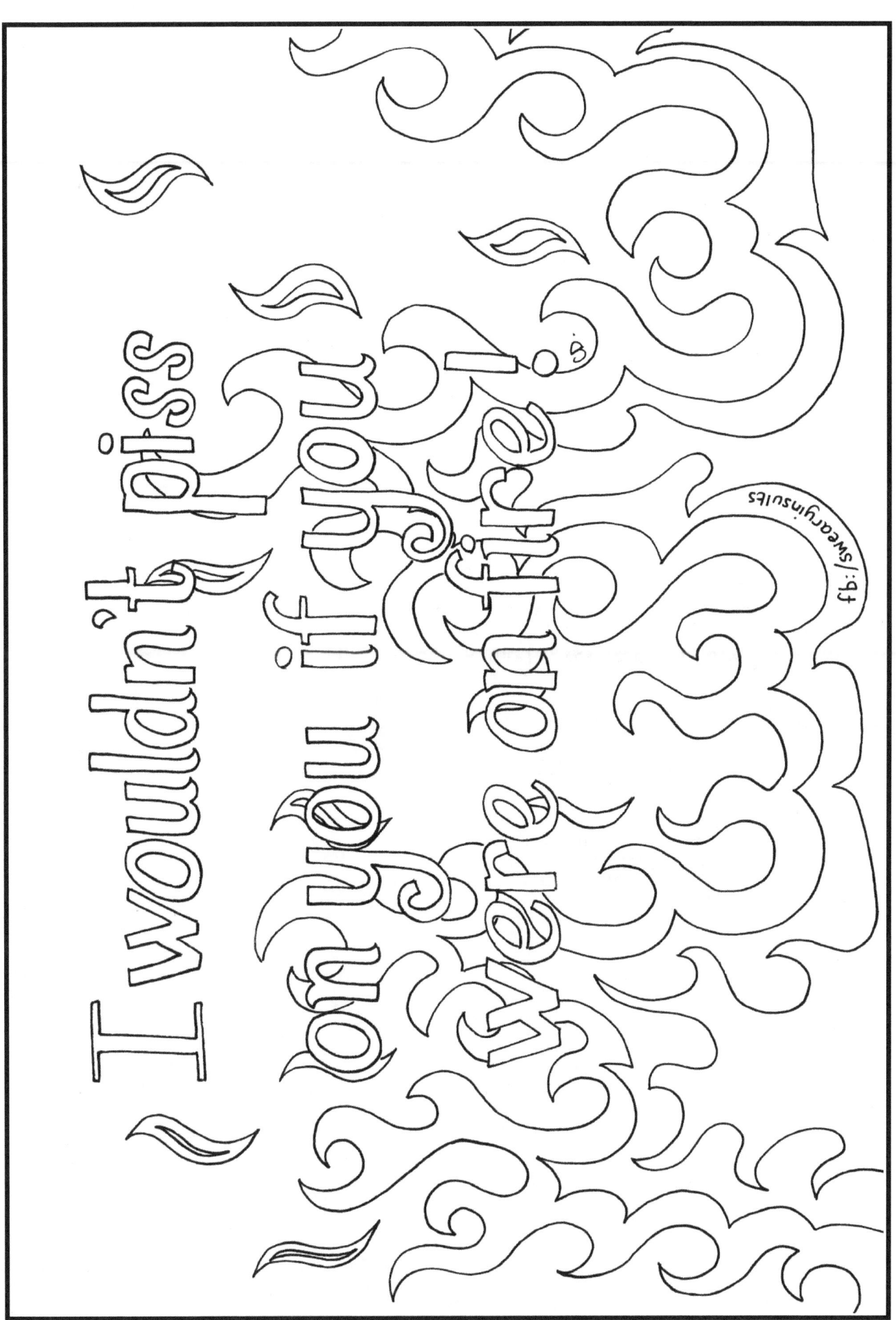

Coloured by:

∘∘∘∘∘∘∘∘∘∘∘∘∘∘∘∘∘∘∘∘∘∘∘

Date:

∘∘∘∘∘∘∘∘∘∘∘∘∘∘∘∘∘∘∘∘∘∘∘

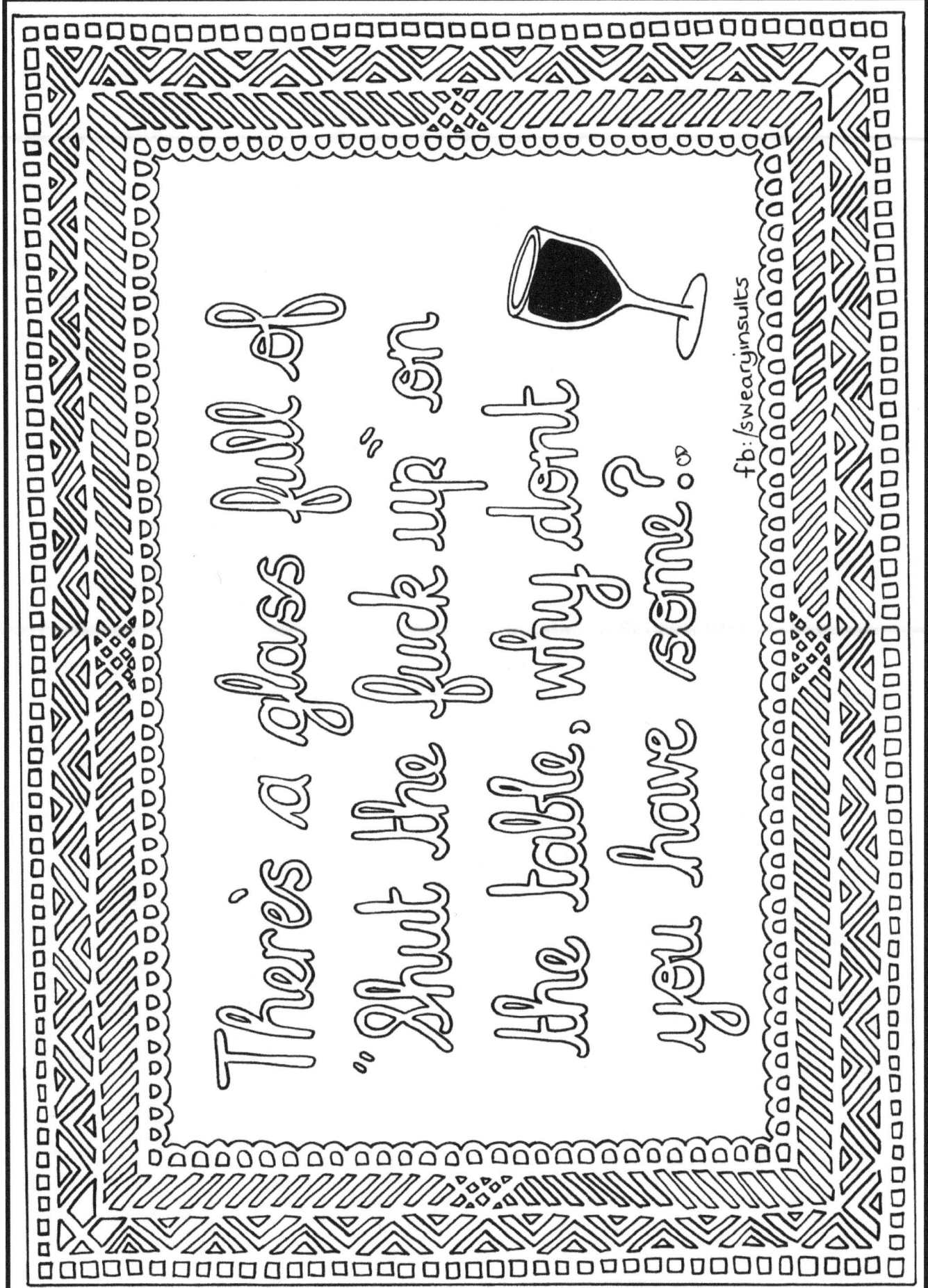

There's a glass full of "Shut the fuck up" on the table, why don't you have some?

fb:/swearyinsults

Coloured by:

○ ○

Date:

○ ○

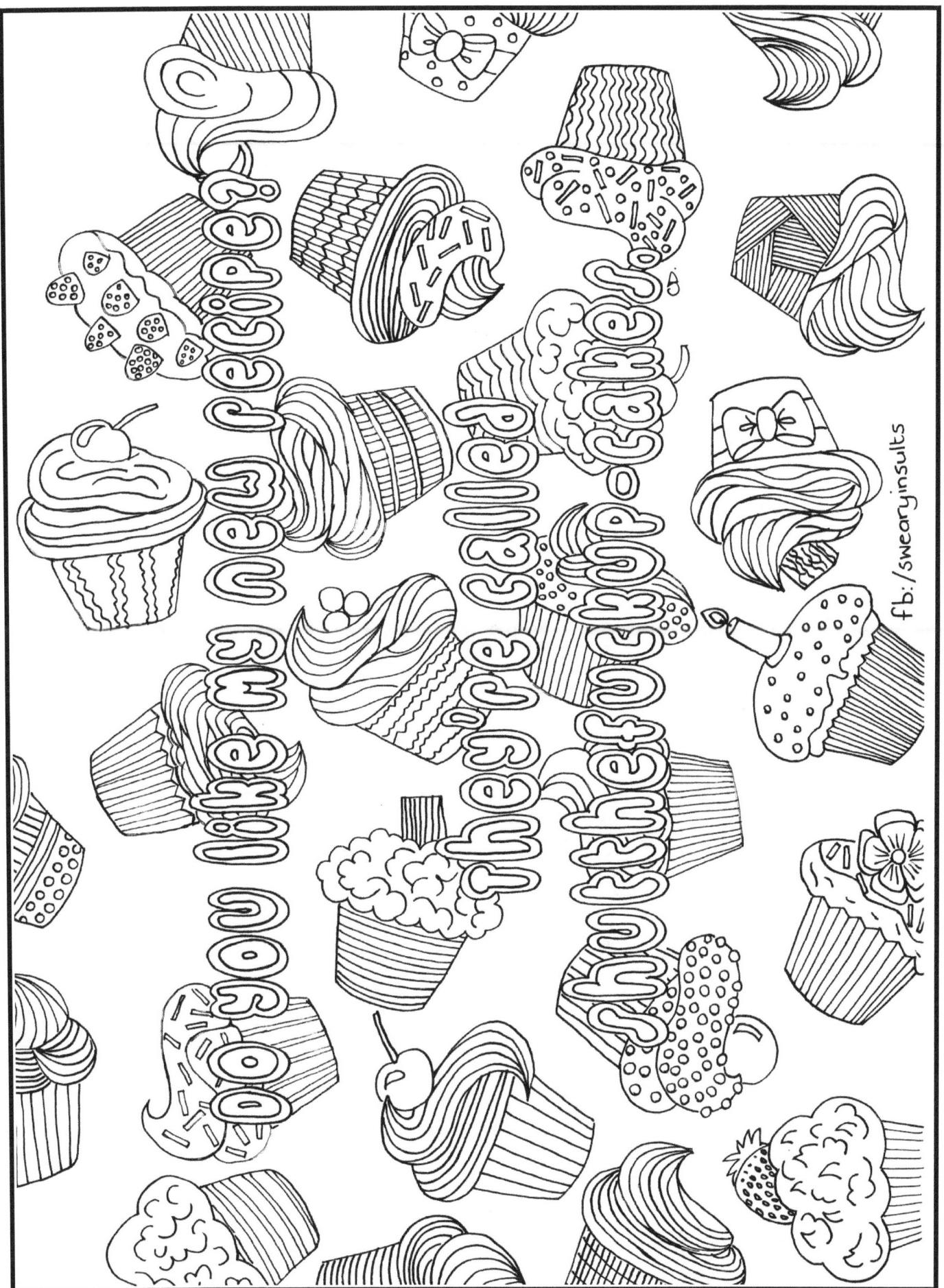

fb:/swearyinsults

Coloured by:

Date:

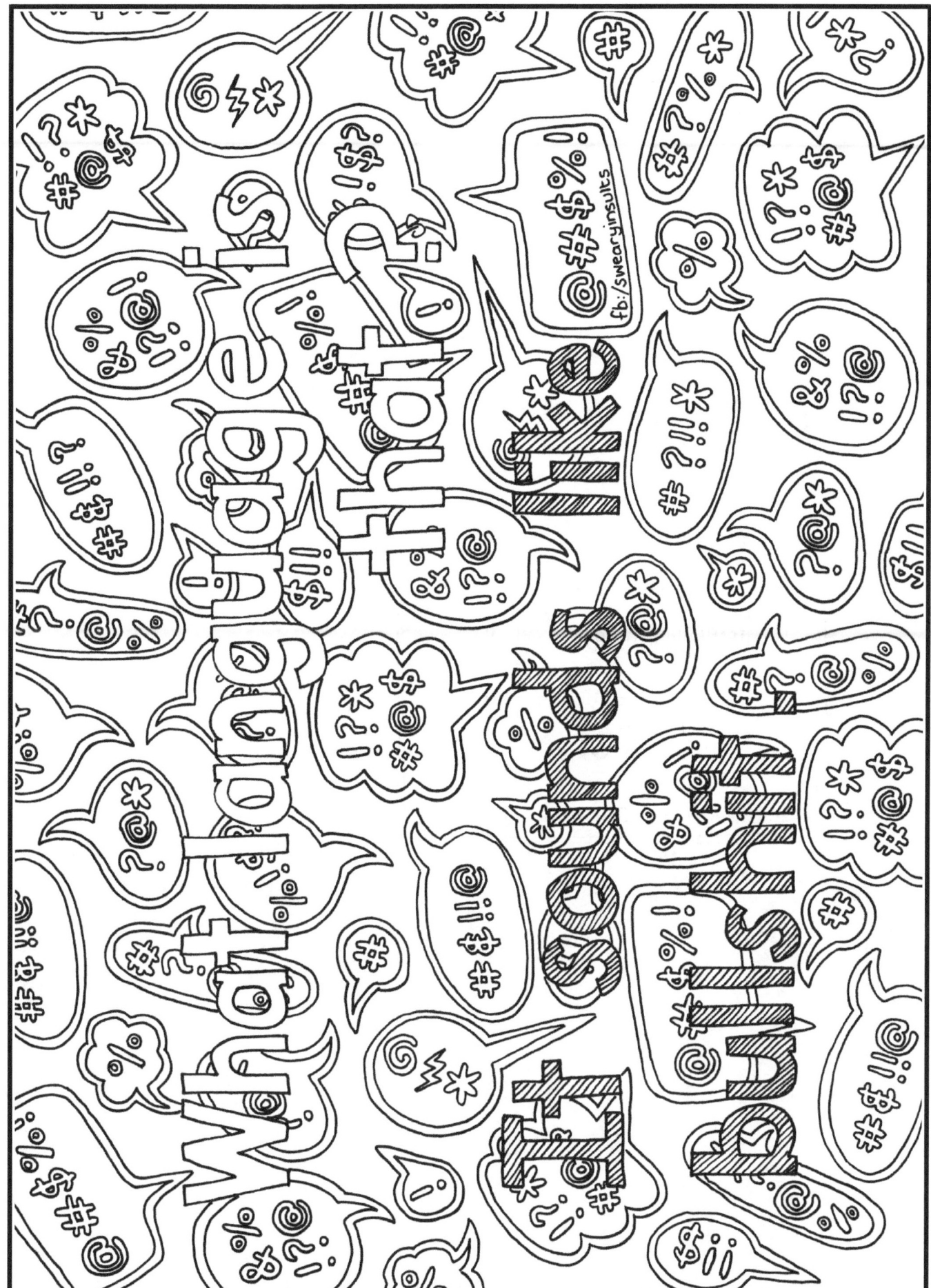

Coloured by:

○ ○

Date:

○ ○

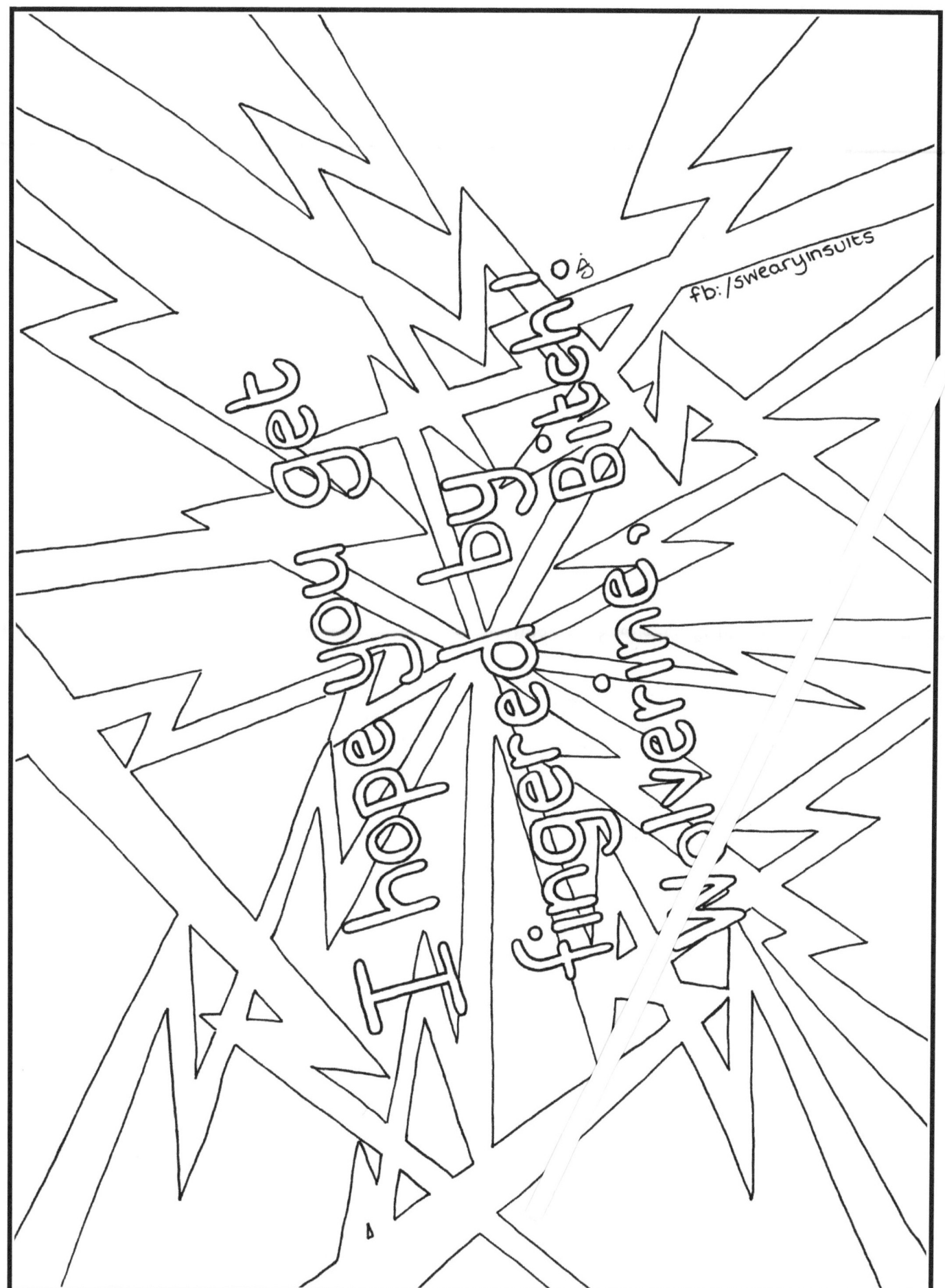

Coloured by:

∘∘∘∘∘∘∘∘∘∘∘∘∘∘∘∘∘∘∘∘∘∘∘∘∘

Date:

∘∘∘∘∘∘∘∘∘∘∘∘∘∘∘∘∘∘∘∘∘∘∘∘∘

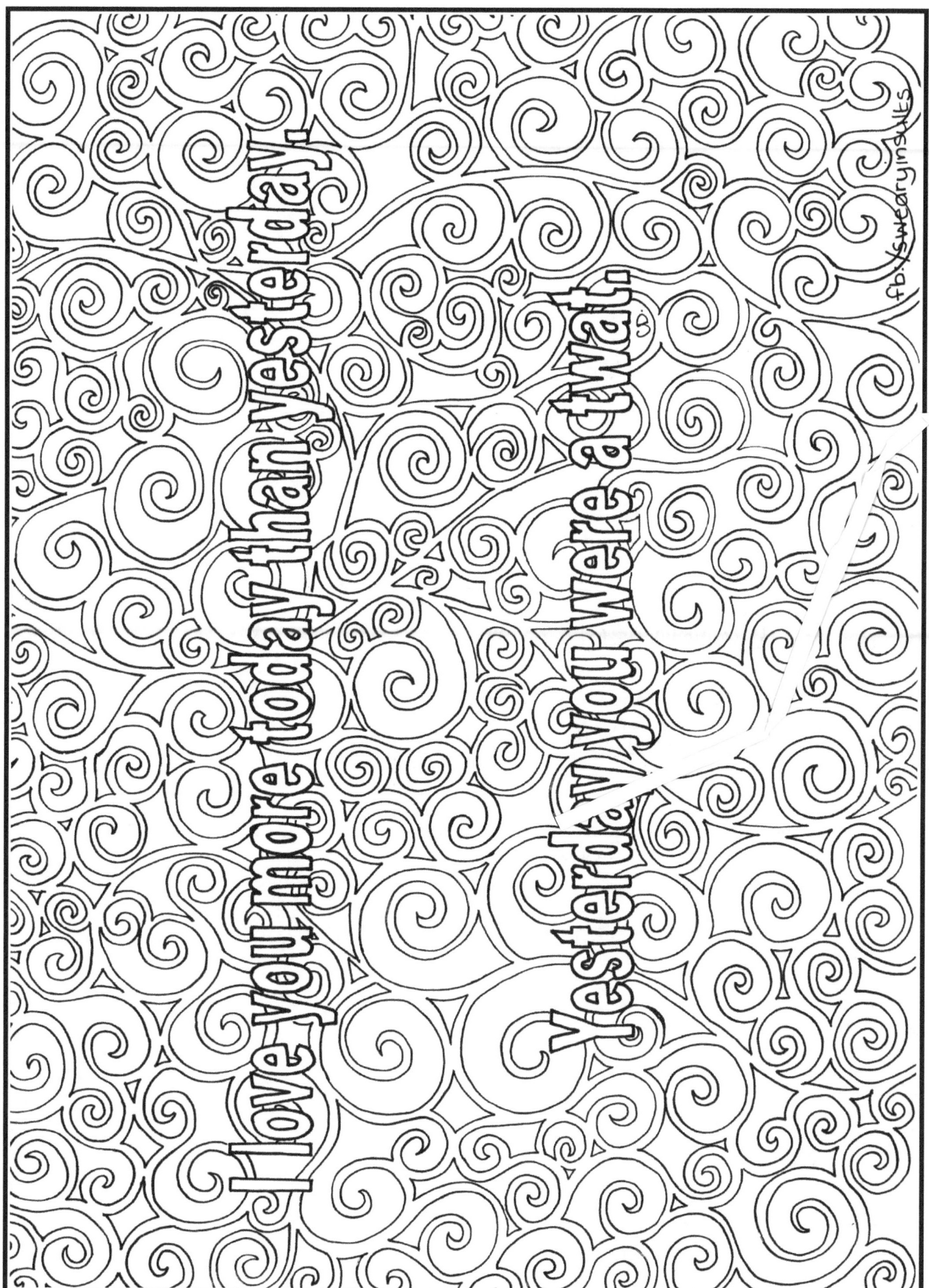

I love you more today than yesterday.

Yesterday you were a twat.

Coloured by:

∘∘∘∘∘∘∘∘∘∘∘∘∘∘∘∘∘∘∘∘∘∘∘∘

Date:

∘∘∘∘∘∘∘∘∘∘∘∘∘∘∘∘∘∘∘∘∘∘∘∘∘

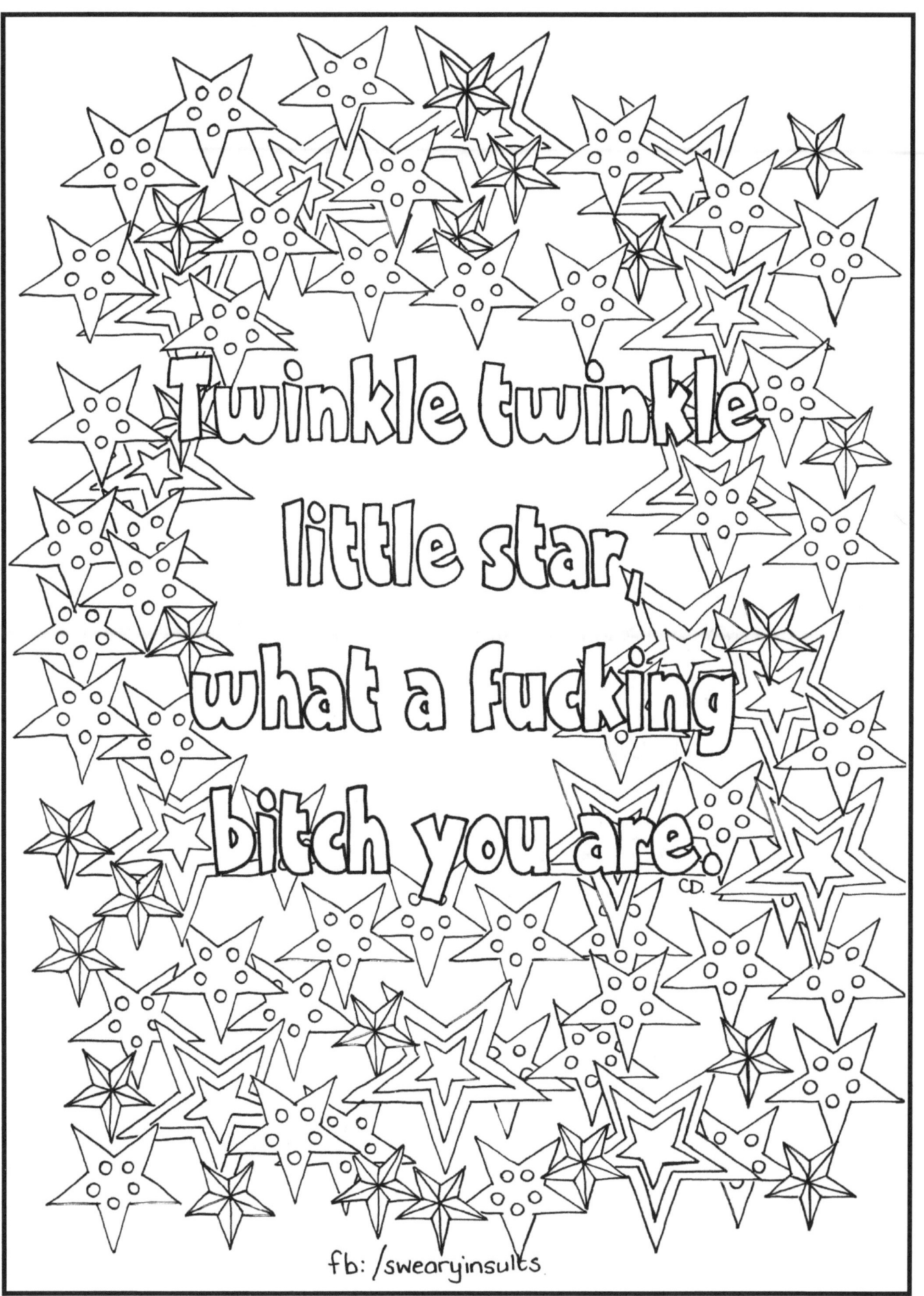

Twinkle twinkle little star, what a fucking bitch you are.

fb: /swearyinsults

Coloured by:

∘∘∘∘∘∘∘∘∘∘∘∘∘∘∘∘∘∘∘∘∘∘

Date:

∘∘∘∘∘∘∘∘∘∘∘∘∘∘∘∘∘∘∘∘∘∘∘

www.ingramcontent.com/pod-product-compliance
Lightning Source LLC
Chambersburg PA
CBHW080626190526
45169CB00009B/3296